Griffin Publishing Group and Teacher Created Materials wish to thank the many talented and devoted supporters of the Olympic Games that made this publication possible.

DIRECTOR OF OPERATIONS	Robin L. Howland	EDITOR	Eric Migliaccio
PROJECT MANAGER	Bryan K. Howland	WRITER	Debra J. Housel, M.S. Ed.
COVER DESIGN	Barb Lorseyedi	ILLUSTRATOR	Bruce Hedges

USOC Officers (2001-2004)

Sandra (Sandy) Baldwin, Chair/President
Paul E. George, Vice Chair
Marty Mankamyer, Secretary

Herman R. Frazier, Vice Chair
Brig. Gen. James (Jim) R. Joy (ret.), Vice Chair
Frank Marshall, Treasurer

USOC Management Staff

Scott Blackmun, Acting Chief Executive Officer
Matt Mannelly, Sr. Managing Director, Marketing
Mike Moran, Managing Director, Media Relations & Programs

10 9 8 7 6 5 4 3 2 1

ISBN 1-58000-078-9

Griffin Publishing Group
2908 Oregon Court, Suite I-5, Torrance, CA 90503
Phone (310) 381-0485
www.griffinpublishing.com
Manufactured in the United States of America

Published in association with and distributed by

Teacher Created Materials
6421 Industry Way
Westminster, CA 92683
www. teachercreated.com

Table of Contents

Table of Contents *(cont.)*

Introduction

Every two years the eyes of the world turn to athletes who compete to see who is the fastest runner, the highest jumper, the speediest skier, the most graceful skater. Top athletes from around the world receive medals signifying that they are the best. This book is about Olympic competition. The official designation, Olympic Games, refers to the games held during the summer every four years. The games held during the winter every four years are officially known as the Olympic Winter Games. This book will provide you with ideas, materials, and activities that can be used with students in grades K–2.

The contents are designed to provide the following:

- information and activities to familiarize students with the Olympics
- creative worksheets that help children to learn about the Olympics while practicing vital skills
- plans for a Junior Olympic Games culminating activity
- teacher resources, including bulletin boards, learning center(s), answer key, relevant Web sites, and a bibliography

These materials are appropriate for:

- class or group lessons
- independent enrichment and research
- cooperative learning activities

The Olympic Winter Games, held in January or February, offer the opportunity for additional activities based on the daily schedules of the Games.

The Olympic Games, held in July, August, or September, may be introduced to the students during the events (if school is in session) or at the end of the traditional school year so that they can better appreciate the Games on television or in person.

The hope for world peace is renewed at each Olympic Games. While the Olympic flag flies and the Olympic flame glows in the cauldron, people everywhere think about world peace and cooperation. As people watch the ceremonies and competitions, they appreciate and respect the incredible talent and dedication of individual athletes. Differences in nationalities pale in comparison to the similarities of the human spirit. The activities in this book will bring the Olympic spirit alive for your students.

Bulletin Board

Create a bulletin board entitled "The Olympic Games Bring the World Together." Display an enlarged version of the world map (on pages 8–9). You can make a transparency by photocopying the pages. Then display the transparency on a blank wall on which you have mounted a large sheet of butcher paper cut to the dimensions of your bulletin board. Move the overhead back until the map fills the butcher paper. Trace the map carefully in pencil; then go over it with a felt-tip marker. If you have enough space, copy the pictograms from pages 10–14. Cut them out and staple them around the bulletin board's border to create a decorative "frame."

Refer to the bulletin board throughout the unit, preferably daily. Place a colored pushpin at your own location. Then when you discuss the current and past Olympic host cities, point out where each one is on the map with a colored pushpin. Use this as an opportunity to discuss geography. For example, you can ask the children what ocean lies between where you live and the city where the Games were held. Each day discuss the winners of the events the prior day. For example, "The Canadians won the gold medal, Russia won the silver medal, and the Germans won the bronze medal in ice hockey last night—let's point out those countries on the map. Why might people in those countries be especially good at ice hockey?"

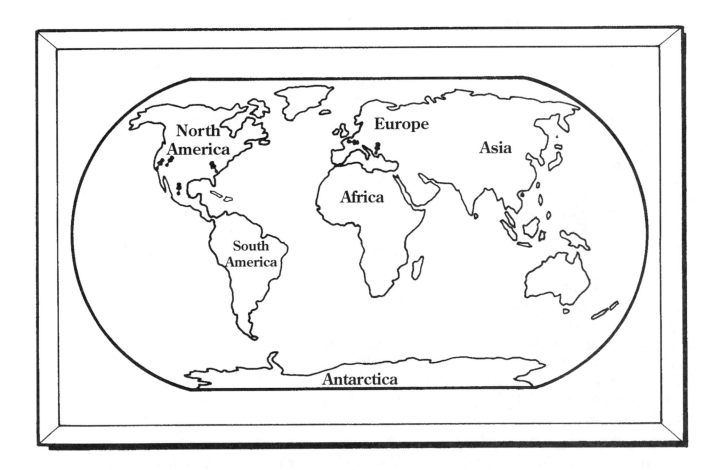

If you want an additional bulletin board, you can also photocopy the pictograms that relate to the current Olympics. Enlarge the pictograms on pages 10–14 with a photocopier. Then have the children color the backgrounds and attach them to the board.

Learning Center Activities

1. **Practice Writing Letters and Words**—Provide salt trays and have the children practice writing Olympic-related words: Olympics, team, sport, play, win, gold medal, etc. You can also have the children spread shaving cream on a desk or table and write the words. Most kids love writing in shaving cream, and the surface ends up cleaner than it started! A third option is to provide prepared butterscotch pudding and have the children write 'gold medal' and draw a gold medal with the pudding on a piece of construction paper. Allow the project to dry thoroughly before sending home. Be sure to provide models for them to look at while writing the words.

2. **Practice with Words**—Provide magnetic, sandpaper, or crepe rubber letters. Be sure to have multiples of frequently used letters, especially a, e, i, l, n, o, r, s, t, u, y. Provide laminated cards on which you have traced these words:

   ☞ Simple words:

• run	• play	• boat
• row	• ball	• ride
• box	• world	• horse
• swim	• snow	• sled
• fun	• ice	• win

   ☞ Basic words (all kindergarten words, plus the following):

• sport	• curl	• gold
• team	• broom	• silver
• shoot	• rock	• bronze
• skate	• house	• medal
• ski	• bike	• Olympics
• pole	• dive	

   ☞ Advanced words:

• biathlon	• basketball	• soccer
• curling	• boxing	• softball
• hockey	• canoe	• swimming
• bobsled	• kayak	• tennis
• luge	• cycling	• handball
• skiing	• diving	• triathlon
• snowboard	• fencing	• volleyball
• speed skating	• gymnastics	• weightlifting
• figure skating	• equestrian	• sailing
• archery	• judo	• wrestling
• athletics	• water polo	• compete
• badminton	• rowing	
• baseball	• shooting	

Draw a small picture on each card so that the children are sure of the word with which they are working. The children use the letters to build the word on the card. Then they should write the word by hand on a blank 3 x 5 card. At the end of the unit, the children can take home their set of 3 x 5 cards and read them to their parents.

Learning Center Activities *(cont.)*

3. **Create a Crown of Olive Leaves**—Use green construction paper and green pipe cleaners (chenille sticks) to create a crown of olive leaves.

4. **Sports Sort for Olympic Games**—Copy, cut, and laminate the sports pictograms from pages 11–14. Place them in the learning center. Provide a large, laminated piece of posterboard with two columns:

   Sports that use a ball   **Sports that need water**

   The children place the pictograms under the correct column. Provide the answer key on a separate card so that the exercise is self-checking.

5. **Sports Sort for Olympic Winter Games**—Copy, cut, and laminate the sports pictograms from pages 10. Place them in the learning center. Provide a large, laminated piece of posterboard with two columns:

   Sports that need snow   **Sports that need ice**

   The children place the pictograms under the correct column. Provide the answer key on a separate card so that the exercise is self-checking.

6. **Class Olympics Book**—Have each child write or draw pages about a favorite Olympic sport to be included in a class book.

7. **Learn About the Flags of Other Nations**—Post colored examples of the world flags from pages 42 and 43. First, cover the country names above the flags on these pages. Then, copy these pages (preferably enlarged) and color them. Laminate the page for durability. Cover the country names above the flags on pages 42 and 43. Then make photocopies. Have the children color the world flags to match the ones in your sample and print the country's name beneath each flag.

8. **Practice Making Patterns**—Provide a model made using the example given below. Reproduce many sheets of reduced-size pictograms from pages 10–14. These pages can be reduced using a photocopier. Cut out the pictograms and group them (using a drawer or cosmetic organizer). Also, provide sheets of construction paper. Have the children glue the pictograms in a repeating pattern of their choice, such as:

As an added challenge for older students, ask them to look at their patterns and then write at least one thing that all the pictures have in common. (In the above example, the pictures all have this in common: all the sports require helmets; all the sports are in the Olympic Summer Games; etc.)

World Map

North
America

South
America

World Map *(cont.)*

Olympic Logos

Winter Sports

Biathlon

Curling

Ice Hockey

Bobsled

Figure Skating

Luge

Skiing

Snowboarding

Speed Skating

Olympic Logos *(cont.)*

Summer Events

Archery

Athletics

Badminton

Baseball

Basketball

Boxing

Canoe/ingKayaking

Cycling

Olympic Logos *(cont.)*

Summary Events *(cont.)*

Diving

Fencing

Gymnastics

Equestrian

Field Hockey

Judo

Modern Pentathlon

Rowing

Olympic Logos *(cont.)*

Summary Events *(cont.)*

Sailing

Shooting

Soccer

Softball

Swimming

Synchronized Swimming

Table Tennis

Taekwondo

Olympic Logos *(cont.)*

Summer Events *(cont.)*

Tennis

Team Handball

Triathlon

Volleyball

Weight Lifting

Water Polo

Wrestling

Felt Board Art

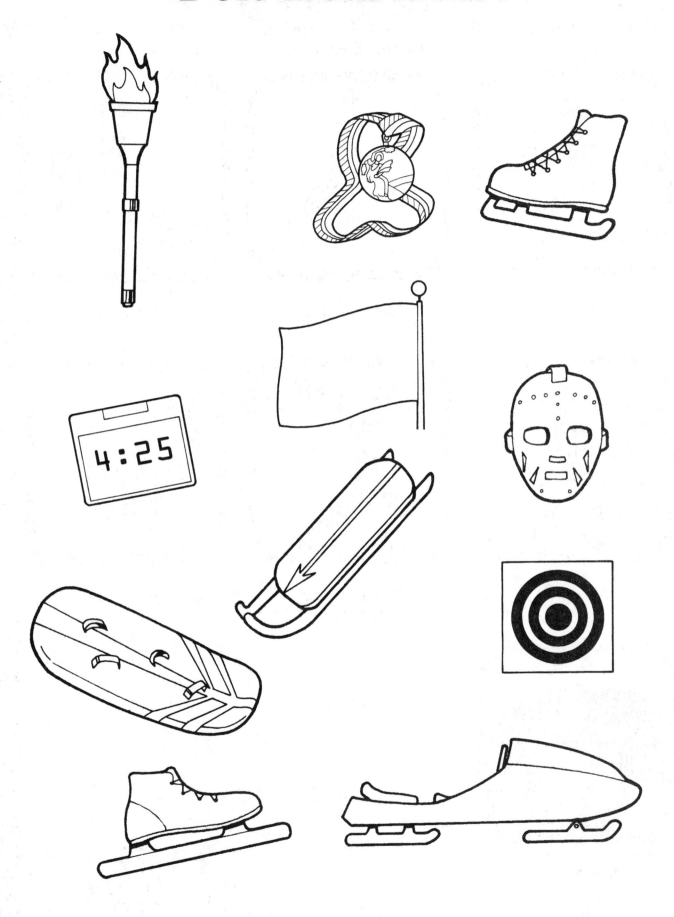

Felt Board Art *(cont.)*

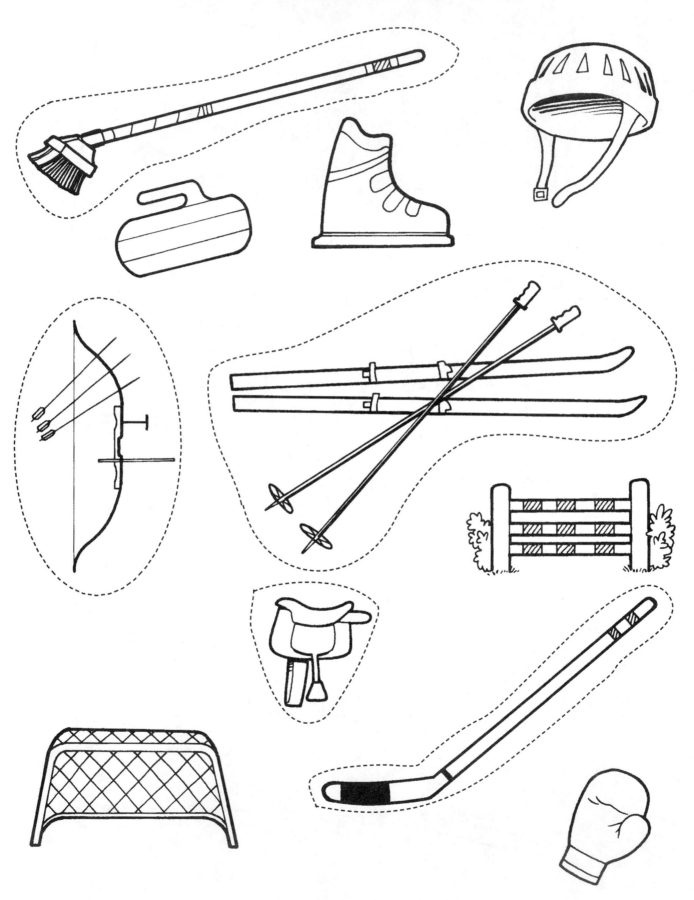

Felt Board Art *(cont.)*

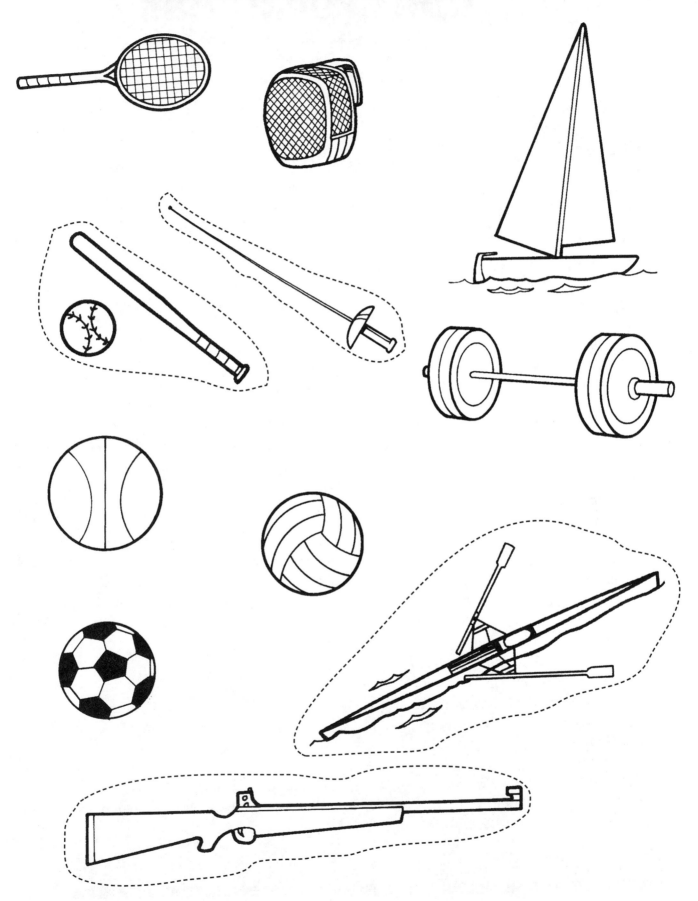

Olympic Vocabulary

There are many words and concepts related to the Olympics with which young children may not be familiar. Introduce and explain these words. Use word walls, charades, felt board, and pocket chart activities to help teach and reinforce Olympics vocabulary.

ancient: very old; from long ago

athlete: a person trained in games or requiring physical skill, endurance, and strength

bronze medal: a round, decorative piece of bronze (metal) given to the third-place winner in each Olympic event

ceremonies: a series of acts performed in a certain way according to fixed rules

closing ceremony: the ceremony that occurs at the end of every Olympics

compete: to try to win a prize or reward

competitors: people who are trying to win the same prize or reward

competition: a contest in which everyone tries to win the same prize or reward

event: a contest in a sports program

flame: a fire that burns in the cauldron at the Olympics as a symbol of peace between the competing nations

gold medal: a round, decorative piece of gold given to the first-place winner in each Olympic event

Greece: the Mediterranean country where the Ancient and Modern Olympics were first held

Olympic Games: a series of international athletic contests held in a different country every four years

Olympic rings: a set of five interlocking, colored, circular bands (also introduce color words for the rings: blue, yellow, black, green, and red)

Olympic Winter Games: a series of international winter-event athletic contests held in a different country every four years (begun in 1924)

opening ceremony: the ceremony that occurs at the start of every Olympics

modern: relating to the present time or time not long past

Paralympics: a series of international athletic contests for the disabled held immediately after every Olympics (begun in 1960)

participants: people who join with others in doing the same thing

participate: to join with others in doing the same thing

play: to take part in a game or exercise

qualify: to show the ability or skills needed to be on a team or to take part in a contest

silver medal: a round, decorative piece of silver given to the second-place winner in each Olympic event

sport: a physical activity engaged in for pleasure rather than necessity

team(s): a group of athletes working together toward a common goal

torch: a flaming light lit by the sun's rays in Greece and carried from there by hand to the Olympic site

USA: United States of America

Word Wall Activities

For younger students . . .

1. Select words from the list on page 23. Write each word on a 4" x 6" card. Post each letter of the alphabet on a wall or board. If your space is limited, post just those letters that will have words beneath them (e.g., leave out x or z if you're not going to have any word cards underneath those letters). Present several words each day, always in alphabetical order. Then have the children tape or pin them underneath the correct letter.

2. Explain rhyme and give some examples (cat, fat, bat, mat, etc.). Then ask the children to think of words that rhyme with the simplest words on the word wall (play, team, gold, event, etc.). Record their answers on chart paper and post in the room.

3. Help the children see how to analyze words by saying, "What word on the wall starts with 'S' and rhymes with fort?" When the children respond, 'sport,' write both words on the board or chart paper. Ask them how the words are the same. Ask them what makes the words different. Have them try to think of words that rhyme with sport and fort (short, sort, port, snort, airport, report, etc.). If they come up with 'court' or 'quart,' write them down. Then explain that sometimes even when words don't look exactly the same, they may still rhyme.

4. To promote higher-level thinking skills, choose a set of cards and ask the children to "sort" the words by:

   • those that contain the same first letter

   • those that contain the same last letter

   • those requiring capitalization vs. those that do not

For older students . . .

1. Select words from the list on page 23. Write each word on a 4" x 6" card. Post each letter of the alphabet on a wall or board. If your space is limited, post just those letters that will have words beneath them (i.e., leave out x or z if you're not going to have any word cards underneath those letters). Present several words each day, always in alphabetical order. Then have the children tape or pin them underneath the correct letter.

2. Have children write sentences using the words, then exchange with a partner and read.

3. Choose a mystery word from the wall. On the board make a blank for each letter. As children take turns guessing a letter, write correct letters in the appropriate blank. The child who correctly guesses or can read the word earns a point. Points can accumulate throughout the unit and prizes can be awarded at the end.

4. Practice learning to spell the words through song. Hold up a word card and sing to the tune of "Frere Jacques:"

We can spell silver;

We can spell silver;

Here's how it's spelled

Here's how it's spelled

S-I-L-V-E-R

That's silver; that's silver.

Word Wall Activities *(cont.)*

For older students . . . *(cont.)*

5. To promote higher-level thinking skills, choose a set of cards and ask the children to "sort" the words by:

   • those that contain the same first letter; those that contain the same last letter
   • those containing long vowels vs. those containing short vowels
   • those requiring capitalization vs. those that do not
   • words that are nouns vs. words that are verbs.

6. To develop listening and analytical skills, play Word Sleuth. Give the children clues to guess a word from the wall.

   Example: Clue 1 "I'm thinking of a word with six letters."
   (Students take a guess.)
   Clue 2 "It has three vowels, and they're all the same."
   (Students take a guess.)
   Clue 3 "It begins with a capital letter."
   (Students will probably guess the word "Greece.")

7. Pair the students. Provide cloze sentences (on board or as worksheet). The pairs need to refer to the word wall to find the word that would fit. Depending on the needs of your students, you can make this less challenging by giving the number of letters in the answer or revealing the initial letter as an added clue.

   Example: The first <u>Olympics</u> were held in Greece.

Charades

After you have introduced the different games of the Olympics, have the children take turns miming an action. Have the rest of the class take guesses as to what the child is doing (skating, curling, swimming, diving). You may want to model this activity for younger students.

Memory Game

Reinforce visual memory and discrimination by creating Olympic memory game cards. Reproduce two sets of pictograms on pages 10–14. Cut apart. Glue winter games on blue oaktag and summer games on yellow oaktag. Laminate for durability.

Olympic Winter Games Memory: Have the children play a memory game by shuffling the blue cards, then laying them out face down in a 6-card by 3-card grid. The children turn over two cards at a time, trying to make a match.

Olympic Games Memory: Have the children play by shuffling the yellow cards, then laying them out face down in an 12-card by 5-card grid. You will need to remove one set so that there will be exactly 60 cards. (If this many cards turns out to be too big of a challenge for your children, either reduce the number of matches or allow the children to play in pairs and consult their partners to help them find the matching card.)

"A" My Name Is Athlete

A fun way to review both the alphabet in sequence and vocabulary concepts is to play a game called "A" My Name is Athlete. Display a large alphabet strip where all can see it. Model the letters A and B by saying: "'A' my name is Athlete, and I'm taking apples to the Olympics. 'B' my name is basketball, and I bounce off a backboard at the Olympics." Point to each letter as you call on a child for the letters C-W, Y and Z. Help a child who might struggle with this activity by calling on her for the initial letter of her first name—that way she can use it for the first part: "'M' my name is Miranda, and I like to watch people win medals at the Olympics." You do the letter X: "'X' my name is excitement, and I bring the world's most excellent athletes to the Olympics."

Traveling Teddy Bear

To help your students learn more about the world and geography, send a teddy bear on a journey. On a 3" x 5" card write this message:

Hi! I'm a member of [your name]'s [your grade] grade class. Please carry me with you on your journey. Send my classmates a postcard or email to let them know where I've been. Then give me to someone else and ask that person to do the same. I need to be returned to [give school's complete postal address and e-mail address] by [give a date that is two months before the end of school]. Thank you for helping my class learn more about the world.

Be sure to include your postal and e-mail addresses on the card. Punch holes in the card's upper corners and thread a ribbon through. Tie the ribbon around the teddy bear's neck. Put the teddy bear into a large, plastic, zipper bag. Do not send a dearly loved teddy bear; often the bears don't get sent back.

Give the bag with the bear to a person who is going on a trip and ask him or her to pass the bear on to another traveler. You'll be amazed at where your bear goes. Whenever you receive messages, share them with the class. Refer to the world map. Ask the students questions such as:

- What continent is our teddy bear on?

- Have the Olympics ever been held on that continent?

- Is our teddy bear in a country that has ever hosted the Olympics?

- What ocean is between us and the teddy bear?

- Who can point out the route the teddy bear probably traveled after his last message?

- Is the teddy bear closer to us or farther away from us than he was last time?

- What language is probably spoken in the place where our teddy bear is?

Pocket Chart Activities

Prepare a pocket chart for storing and using pictograms and word cards. Use a commercial pocket chart, or you can make a pocket chart if you have access to a laminator.

How to Make a Pocket Chart

Begin by laminating a 24" x 36" (61 cm x 91 cm) piece of heavyweight tagboard. To make nine pockets, cut a sheet of clear plastic into nine 2" x 20" (5 cm x 50 cm) strips. Equally space the strips down the 36" (91 cm) length of the tagboard. Attach each strip with clear packing tape along the sides and bottom. This will hold the pictograms and word cards. The pocket chart can be displayed in a learning center or mounted on a chalk tray or easel for use with a group.

How to Use the Pocket Chart

1. Photocopy the pictograms on pages 10–14. Also, make cards for the asterisked items on page 23. Glue them to oaktag and laminate them for durability. On a chalk tray or in a pocket chart, post the pictograms of three events. Discuss each pictogram, asking such questions as the following:

   • Does anyone know what this event is called?

   • Has anyone ever played this sport? (Have volunteers share their experiences.)

   • Has anyone ever watched this sport played (live or on TV)?

2. For younger children, present three events in alphabetical order. For example, present Archery, Basketball, and Cycling. Add to the pocket chart each day, leaving up the events from prior days. After a few days, ask if the students see a pattern. (The sports are being presented in alphabetical order.)

3. For older children, present four or five events not in alphabetical order and ask for volunteers to put the pictograms in alphabetic order. With proficient children, you can give them many pictograms that all share the first letter (snowboarding, speed skating, skiing) and ask a volunteer (or partners) to alphabetize them.

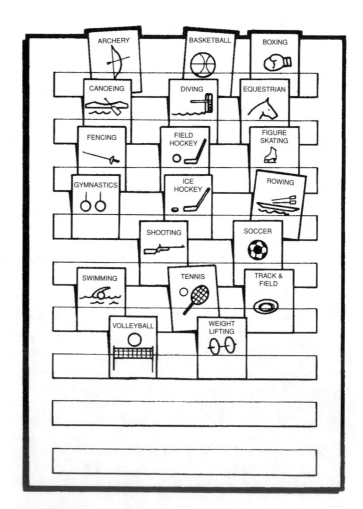

Pocket Chart Activities *(cont.)*

4. This is the alphabetical list. Teacher directions are in italics:

Athletics, archery

Biathlon, basketball, baseball, bobsled, boxing, badminton

Cycling, canoeing, cross-country skiing, curling

Diving

Equestrian

Fencing, field hockey, figure skating

Gymnastics

Hockey *(Compare and contrast field hockey and ice hockey.)*

Ice hockey

Judo

Kayaking

Luge

Marathon

***N**ews

***O**lympic rings or Olympic oath

Pentathlon, pairs skating, paralympics

***Q**ualify *(Explain how an athlete has to win trials to qualify to represent his or her country at the Olympics.)*

Rowing, running

Skiing, snowboarding, speed skating, shooting, swimming, softball, synchronized swimming, sailing

Tennis, taekwondo, team handball, table tennis, triathlon

***U**S Olympic Flag, uneven parallel bars

Volleyball

Water polo, weight lifting, wrestling

***e**X**citing *(Explain that very few words begin with X, and that most words begin with 'ex' when the letter X is pronounced at the beginning.)*

Yell *(Explain that the crowd yells in excitement while the athletes compete.)*

***Z**eus *(mythological Greek god who presided over the Ancient Olympics)*

*In order to cover the complete alphabet, you will need to write these words on 3" x 5" cards.

Felt Board Activities

1. Photocopy the felt board art on pages 15–17. Cut out and color each picture.

2. Glue the pictures to oaktag and laminate them for durability.

3. Attach a piece of Velcro™ or sandpaper to the back of each item.

4. You can buy a felt board or create one by purchasing a piece of felt and gluing it to a large, sturdy piece of cardboard or thin wood.

5. Choose two or three 'sports of the day.' You might want them to correlate to the actual events that are to be played that day (or over the weekend if done on a Friday).

6. During circle time, put the equipment on the felt board in random order. Proceed with these activities:

   • Ask the children to sort the pieces into the sports they go with. Then ask what sport goes with each set of pieces.

   • Discuss why the pieces are needed to play that sport.

   • Have the children determine which pieces are worn by players and which pieces are used by players.

   • Ask the students comparison questions such as, "Which thing is probably the heaviest? lightest? shortest? longest?"

   • If possible, bring in pieces of wood, plastic, fiberglass, metal, and cloth. Pass them around for the children to see and handle. Then ask, "What do you think this [point to thing on the board] is made of? Why do you think it is made from that material?"

   • Ask, "How many sounds do you hear in [point to thing on the board]?" Make sound boxes on the board or chart paper. "How do you think we would spell [point to same thing on the board]?" Fill in the sound boxes on the board or chart paper.

   • "We put the helmet with the [name of sport]. We said that [hockey, ski, bobsled, luge, bike, etc.] players wear helmets. Why do you think this is? When do you wear a helmet?* Why is wearing a helmet important?"

   • Promote oral speaking skills by asking, "Which of these sports (represented by the things on the board) would you most like to participate in? Why?" You want the children to use vocabulary words and formulate a reason why they feel the way they do. So you may need to model an answer, such as: "I would like to be a figure skater. It looks like so much fun to glide around the rink. Skaters always seem to be having a great time dancing to the music."

   • You can also ask, "Are there any of these sports [represented by the things on the board] that you would never want to participate in? Why?" You may need to model an answer, such as: "I'd never want to be a gymnast. The things they do look scary to me. I wouldn't want to do cartwheels on a balance beam."

   *You may need to lead the students to the correct response. The right answer is "Whenever I'm on wheels." Studies have shown that in addition to biking, people should wear a helmet while riding scooters and skateboards and while wearing skates.

Ancient Olympics Mini Book

Materials: copies of pages 26 and 27, construction paper, stapler and staples, and crayons or markers

Procedure:

1. Distribute copies of pages 26 and 27 to each student and have them cut the pages apart.
2. Provide construction-paper covers. Use one of the Olympic rings' colors (black, yellow, blue, green, red), and cut the construction paper to the correct size.
3. Have the children assemble the pages of the book. Check the page order before stapling the covers on the mini books.
4. Hand out crayons or markers. Instruct the students to use them only when you say to do so.
5. Read the script below. Stop at the indicated points to have the children color one of the pages. Repeat this process until you have completed all eight frames.
6. For younger students, do the first four pages one day and use the same procedure to complete the final four pages the next day.
7. Practice choral reading of the mini book at least three times. Also, have the children practice reading it to each other, adult volunteers, or their parents.

The History of the Ancient Olympics

"The Olympic Games began long, long ago in a place far away from our country. These very old Olympics are called ancient, because *ancient* means "long ago." They were very different from the Olympics held today."

☞ **Stop:** Have the children color the background of the title page. Allow about 90 seconds.

"The Olympic Games started in Olympia, Greece in 776 B.C.E.* That was almost 3,000 years ago. The games lasted for five days."

☞ **Stop:** Have the children color page 2. Allow about 90 seconds.

"Only boys and men could play. Women could not even watch the games. That's because the athletes had no clothes on! But in our book, the people will be wearing the clothes of Ancient Greece."

☞ **Stop:** Have the children color page 3. Allow about 90 seconds.

"On Day 1, the athletes chose the games they would play. They promised to play by the rules. The judges promised to be fair, too."

☞ **Stop:** Have the children color page 4. Allow about 90 seconds.

"On Day 2, there was a chariot race. A chariot is a two-wheeled cart pulled by four horses. A man stands inside the cart. Athletes also rode horses, ran foot races, threw spears and discs, and did long jumps."

☞ **Stop:** Have the children color page 5. Allow about 90 seconds.

"On Day 3, all the athletes ate a big feast. After that, boys did foot races, boxing, and wrestling. Only the boys played on Day 3."

☞ **Stop:** Have the children color page 6. Allow about 90 seconds.

"On Day 4, men did boxing, wrestling and more foot races. Only men could play on Day 4 because sometimes they were hurt during the rough events."

☞ **Stop:** Have the children color page 7. Allow about 90 seconds.

"On Day 5 the winners got crowns of olive leaves put on their heads. They were treated as heroes, and when they returned home, big parties were held in their honor."

☞ **Stop:** Have the children color page 8. Allow about 90 seconds.

*(Note: B.C.E. = Before the Common Era)

Ancient Olympics Mini Book *(cont.)*

The Ancient Olympics

2

The first Olympics were held almost 3,000 years ago in Olympia, Greece.

3

Only men and boys could play. Women were not even allowed to watch.

Day 1   4

The athletes picked the games they would play. They promised to play fair.

Ancient Olympics
Mini Book *(cont.)*

Day 2   **5**

There was a chariot race. There were also horse races, foot races, and long jumps.

Day 3   **6**

There was a big meal. Then boys did boxing, wrestling, and foot races.

Day 4   **7**

Men did boxing, wrestling, and more foot races.

Day 5   **8**

The winners put on crowns of olive leaves.

The Ancient Olympic Games

Directions: Draw a crown of olive leaves on the winner's head.

1. Where did the ancient Olympics begin?

2. When were the first Olympics?

3. Who played in the ancient Olympic games?

4. Name three ancient Olympic events.

5. What did the winners get for a prize?

> **For younger students:** Answer first three questions.
> **For older students:** Answer all five questions.

Modern Olympics Mini Book

Materials: copies of pages 30 and 31, construction paper, stapler and staples, and crayons or markers

Procedure:

1. Distribute copies of pages 30 and 31 to each student and have them cut the pages apart.
2. Provide construction-paper covers. Use one of the Olympic rings' colors (black, yellow, blue, green, red), and cut the construction paper to the correct size.
3. Have the children assemble the book. Check the page order before stapling on the covers.
4. Hand out crayons or markers. Instruct the students to use them only when you say to do so.
5. Read the script below. Stop at the indicated points to have the children color one of the pages. Repeat this process until you have completed all eight frames.
6. For younger students, do the first four pages one day and use the same procedure to complete the final four pages the next day.
7. Practice choral reading of the mini book at least three times. Also, have the children practice reading it to each other, adult volunteers, or their parents.

The History of the Modern Olympics

"The Olympic Games began long ago in Ancient Greece. For more than 1,000 years, men and boys played in the Games. But then Greece was destroyed in a war. Over time, people forgot about the Olympics."

☞ **Stop:** Have the children color the background of the title page. Allow about 90 seconds.

"Then a man named Baron Pierre de Coubertin decided to restart the Olympic Games. He thought it would help people all over the world to become friends. He made the Olympic symbol of five rings to show the five participating continents. He counted North and South America as a single continent, which he called the Americas. [Point out these continents to the children: North America, South America, Europe, Asia, Africa, and Australia]. He picked the ring colors because each nation's flag has at least one of these colors."

☞ **Stop:** Have the children color page 2. Allow about 90 seconds.

"In 1896 the first modern Olympic Games were held in Athens, Greece. Ten countries sent athletes. The United States of America won the most gold medals."

☞ **Stop:** Have the children color page 3. Allow about 90 seconds.

"In 1900 women began to compete in the Olympic Games. Their event was lawn tennis. Today women compete in almost every Olympic sport."

☞ **Stop:** Have the children color page 4. Allow about 90 seconds.

"In 1924 the first Olympic Winter Games were held in France. Figure skating and ice hockey were the main events."

☞ **Stop:** Have the children color page 5. Allow about 90 seconds.

"No Olympic Games were held during World War I and World War II. That's because most of the countries were fighting with each other."

☞ **Stop:** Have the children color page 6. Allow about 90 seconds.

"Today Winter or Summer Games are held every two years. The host cities are different each time. The Olympic torch is carried from Greece to the host city."

☞ **Stop:** Have the children color page 7. Allow about 90 seconds.

"Almost 200 countries send athletes to these Winter or Summer Games. The athletes hope to win gold, silver, or bronze medals."

☞ **Stop:** Have the children color page 8.

Modern Olympics Mini Book *(cont.)*

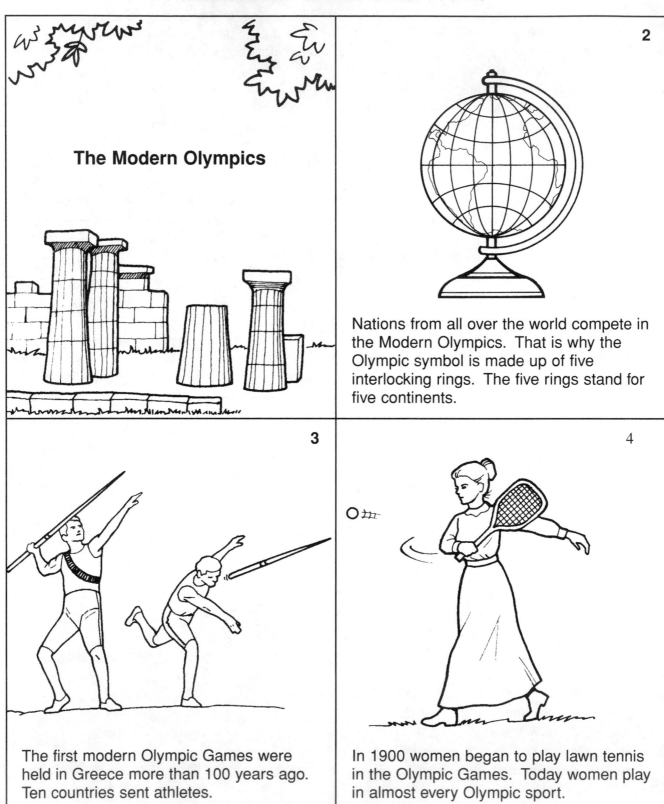

2

The Modern Olympics

Nations from all over the world compete in the Modern Olympics. That is why the Olympic symbol is made up of five interlocking rings. The five rings stand for five continents.

3

The first modern Olympic Games were held in Greece more than 100 years ago. Ten countries sent athletes.

4

In 1900 women began to play lawn tennis in the Olympic Games. Today women play in almost every Olympic sport.

Modern Olympics
Mini Book *(cont.)*

5

In 1924 the first Olympic Winter Games were held in France.

6

No Olympic Games were held during World War I and World War II. That's because most of the countries were fighting with each other.

7

Today Winter or Summer Games are held every two years in different host cities. A torch is carried from Greece to the host city.

8

Almost 200 countries send athletes to the Olympics. The athletes hope to win medals.

Making the Olympic Rings

This project provides an enjoyable way for your children to recognize the Olympic rings, which are the official symbol of the Olympic Games. It would be best to display a finished model before beginning this project. This will get the kids excited about doing the project and help them to understand what they need to do. The project will take six sessions to complete.

Materials:

- sturdy piece of cardboard or a sheet of poster board for each child
- tempera paints in blue, yellow, black, green, and red
- painting smock for each child
- paint brush for each child
- white glue for each child
- water in a can on each table
- ring pattern on cardstock (from page 33)
- 1 bag of rice for every 3 children

Procedure:

1. For each child, draw five interlocking Olympic rings on a piece of cardboard or sheet of poster board. (Trace around the ring pattern from page 33, being certain to interlock the rings correctly.)

2. Pass out a prepared board and rice and white glue to each child.

3. Have the children use paintbrushes to spread glue around each circle. Emphasize that they are to follow the circles on the paper and not fill them in.

4. Have the children immediately rinse their paintbrushes in the water cans as soon as they are done spreading the glue.

5. Ask the children to press the rice onto the outline of the rings. Have those who finish quickly assist others. Let the projects dry overnight.

6. The next day discuss with the children the concepts of *over*, *under*, and *through*. Show and discuss how the blue and yellow rings relate to each other using these terms. Then have children paint the first rice ring blue. Let it dry overnight.

7. The next day, review with the children the concepts of *over*, *under*, and *through*. Show and discuss how the yellow and black rings relate to each other using these terms. Have the children paint the second ring yellow. Let it dry overnight.

8. Have the children paint the third ring black. Let it dry overnight. The children should paint the fourth ring green and the next day paint the last ring red. Each day discuss how the ring the children are to paint that day passes *over*, *under*, and *through* its neighboring ring.

The Olympic Rings

Display a colored set of Olympic rings for children.

Directions: Color the rings in the right order.

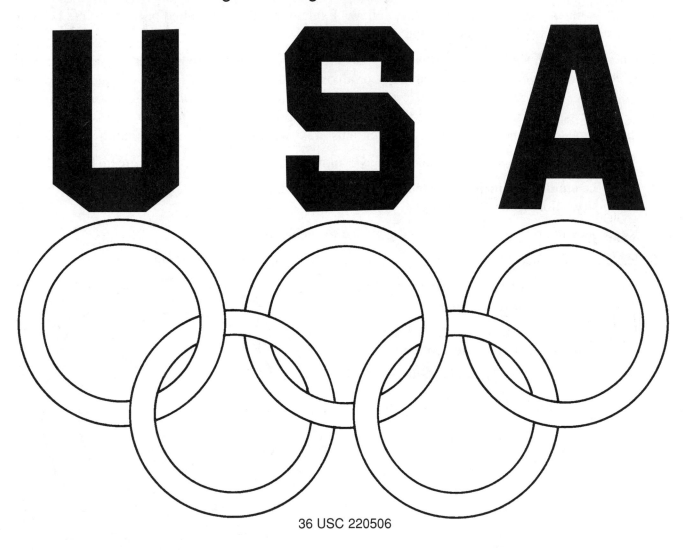

36 USC 220506

For younger students: Write the color words inside each ring.

For older students: Write the color words inside each ring. Write a sentence that tells how the colors for the Olympic rings were picked.

Creating and Reading a Pictograph

1. Discuss the primary colors: red, blue, yellow. Explain that they are called primary colors because you cannot mix two other colors and get them.

2. On an overhead, show how overlaying a yellow transparency on a blue transparency makes green. If you do not have colored transparencies or an overhead, you can tape a piece of blue cling wrap to a blank transparency. Tape a piece of yellow cling wrap to another blank transparency. Hold each transparency up to a window; then overlay the yellow on the blue to form green. Explain that green is a secondary color because you must mix two colors (yellow and blue) to create it.

3. Show the children a colored sample of the Olympic rings (blue, yellow, black, green, and red).

4. Have the children identify the primary colors in the Olympic rings (red, blue, yellow) and the secondary colors (green and black).

5. Reproduce the ring pattern below and give one to each child.

6. Have each child color the ring his or her favorite Olympic ring color and cut it out.

7. Post a large sheet of butcher paper with the heading "Our Favorite Olympic Colors."

8. Draw five columns beneath. Put a different colored ring at the top of each column.

9. Have each child come up and tape his or her ring under the appropriate column.

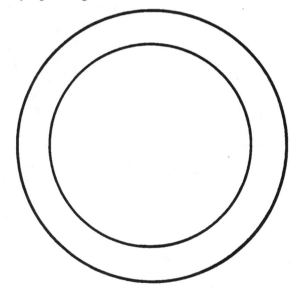

For younger students: With the class, count the number of rings in each row and answer these questions:

- Which color is the most popular?
- Which color is the least popular?
- Are there any colors that no one chose?
- How many more students chose [color] than [color]?
- If [another teacher in your grade]'s class made a chart, would it be the same as ours? Why or why not?

For older students: Have students write the answers to the questions above.

The Olympic Torch

About two months before the start of the Olympics, a torch is lit in Athens, Greece. The torch is carried all the way to the host city. It is used to light the Olympic flame at the opening ceremony.

Directions: Color the torch.

1 = yellow
2 = orange
3 = black
4 = purple

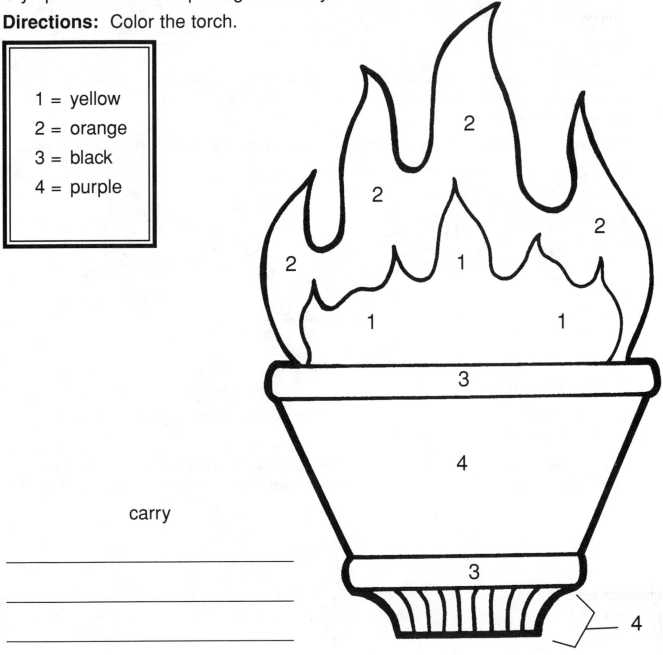

carry

_____

_____

_____

| For younger students: | Write three words that rhyme with carry. |

For younger students: Write three words that rhyme with carry.
For older students: Write three words that rhyme with carry. Write the name of the host city for the Olympics beside the torch.

Olympic Ceremonies

The Opening Ceremony

Inside the Olympic stadium, the host city has dancing and music to start the Olympic Games. Then athletes march into the stadium. One person on each team holds their nation's flag. The Greek athletes always lead the parade. Others follow in A-B-C order by country name. The host country's team is always last.

There is a speech. Often there is entertainment. A flock of white doves is let go. They fly out of the stadium. Then an athlete takes the Olympic torch and lights the Olympic flame in the cauldron. It will burn until the Games are over.

An athlete from the host country leads the athletes in saying the Olympic oath. Everyone promises to play fair.

The Closing Ceremony

The Olympics last for 16 days. Then the athletes return to the stadium to say goodbye. Some have won medals. Many have made new friends.

People from the host country give speeches. Then the flag of the next Olympic host country is raised. The Olympic flame is put out. The Olympic flag comes down. There is music, dancing, and fireworks.

For younger students: Read this page to your class.

For older students: Read this page to your partner. Listen as your partner reads it to you.

The Olympic Flame

The Olympic torch is used to light the Olympic flame at the opening ceremony. The Olympic flame will burn in a cauldron until the closing ceremony.

Directions: Connect the dots in A-B-C order.

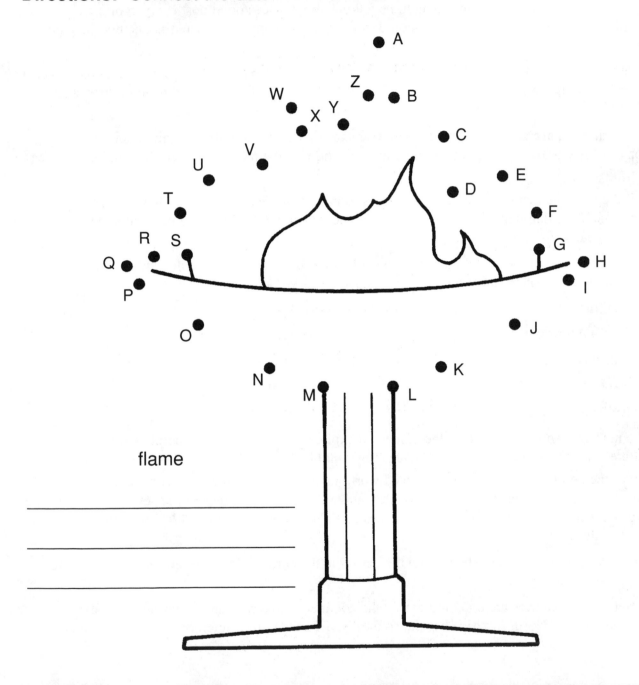

flame

_____

_____

_____

Learn about the World's Continents

1. Tell your students, "Since the Olympics involve athletes from all over the world and have been held all over the world, we are going to be talking about places on almost every continent." Emphasize to the children that they should memorize the names of the continents, not the names or locations of all the countries you point out or discuss.

2. Photocopy the world map on pages 8 and 9. Tape the world map together and use a photocopier to reduce it until it fits on a transparency. Also make copies of the reduced page to distribute to students.

3. If you do not have access to an overhead, you can still do this activity by making an enlarged copy of the world map on pages 8 and 9 and posting it in the room where all the children can see it.

4. Tell the students that even though the earth is round and mountains are tall, they are still represented on flat maps. Display the transparency on an overhead projector. Label the two major oceans (Atlantic and Pacific).

5. Hand out copies of the world map to each student. Ask the students to color the continents on their maps at the same time and with the same color as you do.

6. On the transparency, color each continent with a transparency pen:
   - **North America:** brown
   - **South America:** red
   - **Asia:** yellow
   - **Europe:** purple
   - **Africa:** green
   - **Australia:** orange
   - **Antarctica:** blue

7. The next day, show the students the globe and explain that the earth is sometimes shown as a sphere. Ask for volunteers to locate each continent on the globe.

8. Cover the continent names on the reduced world map page and make photocopies. Pair the students. Give each pair a paper on which you have written the names of the seven continents and two oceans. Ask them to cut apart the names and glue them in the correct location on a blank copy of the world map.

   For older students: Have them write the names in the correct places, referring to the sheet for proper spelling.

9. Explain that countries are on continents. One continent can have many countries. For example, the continent of North America has the countries of Canada, the United States of America, and Mexico.

Olympic Hosts

Year	Olympic Games	Olympic Winter Games
1896	Athens, Greece	***
1900	Paris, France*	***
1904	St. Louis, Missouri, USA	***
1908	London, England (Great Britain)	***
1912	Stockholm, Sweden	***
1916	Not held due to World War I	***
1920	Antwerp, Belgium	***
1924	Paris, France	Chamonix, France
1928	Amsterdam, the Netherlands	St. Moritz, Switzerland
1932	Los Angeles, California, USA	Lake Placid, New York, USA
1936	Berlin, Germany	Garmisch-Partenkirchem, Germany
1940	Not held due to World War II	Not held due to World War II
1944	Not held due to World War II	Not held due to World War II
1948	London, England (Great Britain)	St. Moritz, Switzerland
1952	Helinski, Finland	Oslo, Norway
1956	Melbourne, Australia	Cortina, Italy
1960	Rome, Italy	Squaw Valley, California, USA
1964	Tokyo, Japan	Innsbruck, Austria
1968	Mexico City, Mexico	Grenoble, France
1972	Munich, West Germany	Sapporo, Japan
1976	Montreal, Canada	Innsbruck, Austria
1980	Moscow, Russia	Lake Placid, New York, USA
1984	Los Angeles, California, USA	Sarajevo, Yugoslavia
1988	Seoul, South Korea	Calgary, Canada
1992	Barcelona, Spain	Albertville, France
1996	Atlanta, Georgia, USA	Lillehammer, Norway (1994)
2000	Sydney, Australia	Nagano, Japan (1998)
2004	Athens, Greece	Salt Lake City, Utah, USA (2002)
2008		Torino, Italy (2006)

*First time women competed in the modern Olympics; they played lawn tennis.

***Olympic Winter Games began in 1924.

Flags of Past Olympic Host Countries

Directions: Color the flags.

R = red   G = green   B = blue   W = white

1.

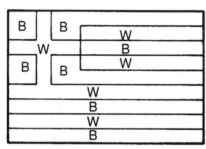

2.

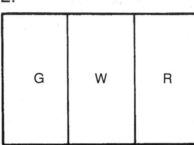

3.

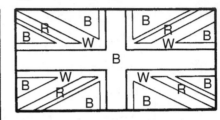

4.

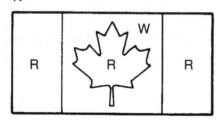

5.

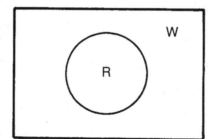

6.

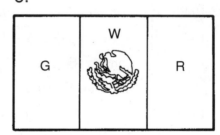

Clue	**Flag Number**
Italy's flag is red, white, and green.	_____
Canada's flag has a red maple leaf on it.	_____
Japan's flag has a red sun.	_____
Great Britain's flag is red, white, and blue.	_____
Mexico's flag has a bird.	_____
Greece's flag has a cross and stripes.	_____

> **For younger students:** Write one of the colors in each flag under the flag.
> **For older students:** Read the clues and write the flag numbers.

National Anthems of Past Olympic Host Countries

Materials:

- enlargements of flags from pages 42–43, colored correctly
- bulletin board of world map
- encyclopedia or books about countries of the world
- compact disc(s)* or cassette(s) with the national anthems of the countries which have hosted the Olympics in the past:

❏ Australia	❏ Finland	❏ France	❏ Italy
❏ Greece	❏ The Netherlands	❏ Switzerland	❏ Austria
❏ England	❏ Mexico	❏ Spain	❏ Japan
❏ Sweden	❏ Russia	❏ Germany	❏ Canada
❏ Belgium	❏ Norway	❏ USA	

Procedure:

1. Have a pushpin on the world map bulletin board in the approximate location of your town or city.
2. Play the national anthem of a country for the class.
3. Show them the flag for that country.
4. Ask a child to put a pushpin on the world map bulletin board (point out the location of the country).
5. Ask the class what kind of Olympics (Summer or Winter) are probably held in that country. Why?
6. The country is a part of which continent?
7. Ask the children which ocean is between the America's western (or eastern) coast and that particular country.
8. Ask if anyone has ever been to the country. Have the child share his or her experience with the rest of the class.
9. From a book or encyclopedia, read to the children a short summary about the country.
10. Do this with at least one country every day of your Olympic unit.

World Anthems performed by Donald Fraser, English Chamber Orchestra. Audio CD (1 disc). BMG/RCA Victor, 63231, 1998. AISN: B000007QGU. (includes the Olympic theme song and the anthems of all of the countries listed above (except Russia or Switzerland))

National Anthems of the World performed by Swarovski Musik Wattens. Audio CD (2 discs). Koch International, 340872, 1996. ASIN: B00000150E. (includes the anthems of all the countries listed above, but does not have Olympic theme song)

Host Country Flags

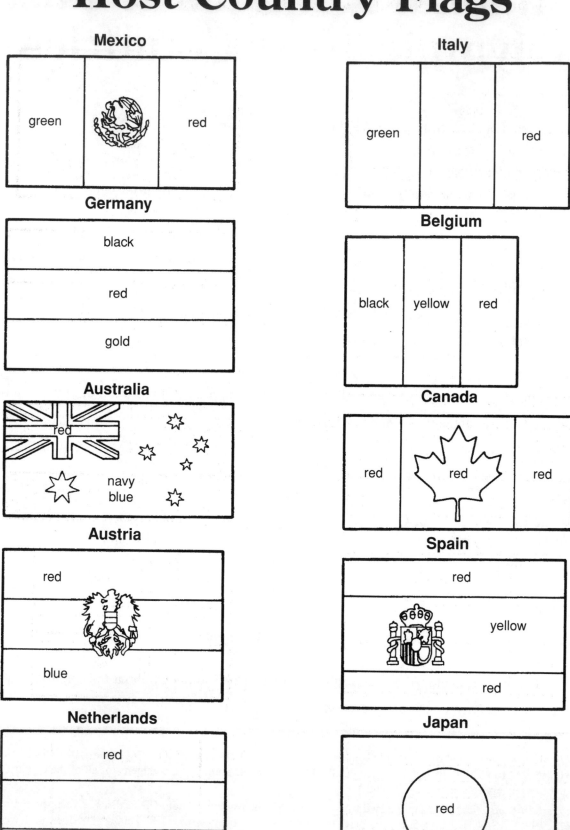

Mexico
green | red

Italy
green | red

Germany
black
red
gold

Belgium
black | yellow | red

Australia
red
navy blue

Canada
red | red | red

Austria
red
blue

Spain
red
yellow
red

Netherlands
red
blue

Japan
red

Host Country Flags *(cont.)*

USSR (Russia)
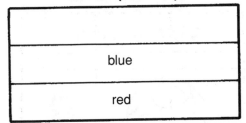

France
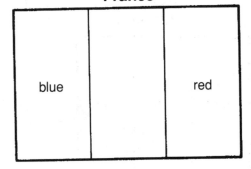

USA
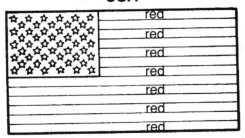

Sweden
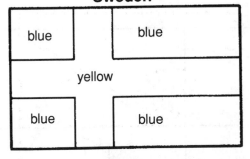

Greece
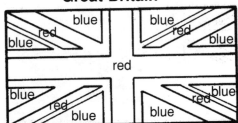

South Korea
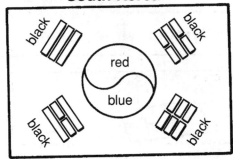

Finland
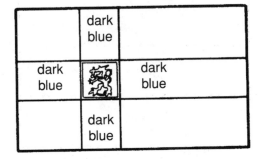

Great Britain
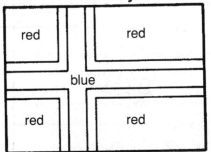

Norway
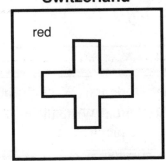

Switzerland

Olympic Sort

Directions: Cut and glue the pictures under the correct Olympics.

Olympic Winter Games	Olympic Games

 L

 B

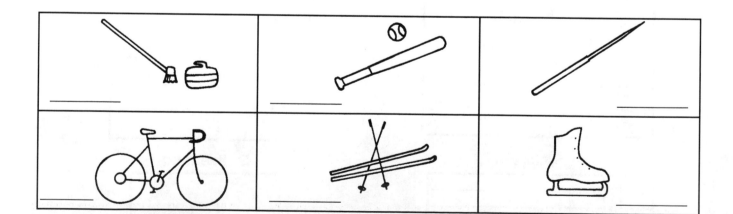

For younger students: Write the beginning sound on the line.

For older students: Write the beginning sound on the line and write two sentences on the back about two of the pictures.

Olympic Sports

Teacher Instructions: Reproduce reduced-size pictograms from pages 10–14 for students. These pages can be reduced using a copier.

Directions: Cut out the pictures. Glue them under the correct heading.

Olympic Sports I Play	Olympic Sports I Watch

For younger students: Draw a line under each vowel in the sports' names. Write a sentence about a sport you play or watch.

For older students: Next to each picture write whether it is a Summer or a Winter Olympics sport. Write a sentence about a sport you play or a sport you watch.

Olympic Addition

Directions: Add. Each answer has a letter. Put the letters on the lines that match the answers. You will find a message.

1. 8 + 4 = _____ F

2. 7 + 7 = _____ T

3. 4 + 7 = _____ O

4. 5 + 5 = _____ E

5. 7 + 6 = _____ R

6. 3 + 8 = _____ O

7. 8 + 8 = _____ G

8. 9 + 8 = _____ D

9. 9 + 9 = _____ L

10. 7 + 9 = _____ G

11. 6 + 5 = _____ O

12. 8 + 7 = _____ H

$\overline{16}$ $\overline{11}$ $\overline{12}$ $\overline{11}$ $\overline{13}$ $\overline{14}$ $\overline{15}$ $\overline{10}$ $\overline{16}$ $\overline{11}$ $\overline{18}$ $\overline{17}$

Olympic Subtraction

Directions: Subtract. Each answer has a letter. Put the letters on the lines that match the answers. With the clues, you will learn the Olympic motto.

1. $1 - 1 =$ _____ S
2. $10 - 2 =$ _____ H
3. $8 - 7 =$ _____ R
4. $4 - 0 =$ _____ G
5. $7 - 4 =$ _____ I
6. $9 - 4 =$ _____ T
7. $7 - 0 =$ _____ F
8. $8 - 6 =$ _____ E
9. $6 - 5 =$ _____ R
10. $10 - 0 =$ _____ N

11. $9 - 5 =$ _____ G
12. $8 - 0 =$ _____ H
13. $10 - 1 =$ _____ O
14. $5 - 0 =$ _____ T
15. $6 - 0 =$ _____ W
16. $5 - 4 =$ _____ R
17. $4 - 2 =$ _____ E
18. $7 - 6 =$ _____ R
19. $6 - 3 =$ _____ I
20. $6 - 4 =$ _____ E

$$\overline{}\ \overline{}\ \overline{}\ \overline{}\ \overline{}\ \overline{}\ \overline{},$$
$$0 \quad 6 \quad 3 \quad 7 \quad 5 \quad 2 \quad 1$$

$$\overline{}\ \overline{}\ \overline{}\ \overline{}\ \overline{}\ \overline{},$$
$$8 \quad 3 \quad 4 \quad 8 \quad 2 \quad 1$$

$$\overline{}\ \overline{}\ \overline{}\ \overline{}\ \overline{}\ \overline{}\ \overline{}\ \overline{}.$$
$$0 \quad 5 \quad 1 \quad 9 \quad 10 \quad 4 \quad 2 \quad 1$$

For older students: Write what you think the Olympic motto means.

When Are the Olympics Held?

Directions: Color the months for the Olympic Winter Games blue.

Color the months for the Olympic Games yellow.

January	February	March	April

May	June	July	August

September	October	November	December

For younger students: Under each colored month, write the name of an Olympic event held then.

For older students: Under each colored month, write the name of an Olympic event held then. Write one sentence telling why the Winter Olympics are held during those months. Write another sentence telling why the Olympic Games are held during those months.

Running at the Olympic Games

Directions: Cut out the pictures. Glue them on another paper in the right order.*

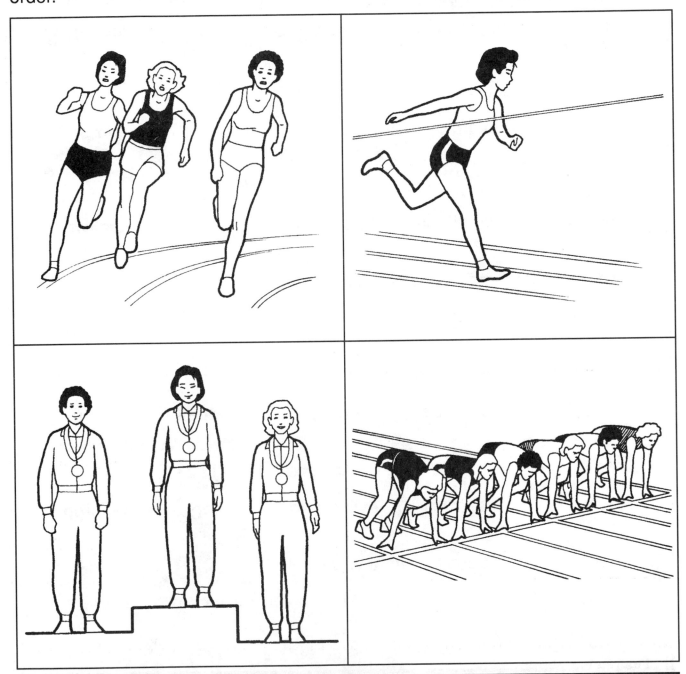

For younger students: Write a caption under each picture.

For older students: Write four sentences that tell the story in the order in which it happened.

*You may prefer to have the children use these pages to create a mini book.

Words from the Olympic Games

Directions: Count the letters in each word.

1. Circle the longest word.

   archery   **badminton**   **gymnastics**   **tennis**   **handball**

2. Circle the shortest word.

   dive   **swim**   **shoot**   **row**   **jump**

3. Circle the word that has a different number of letters.

   pentathlon   **volleyball**   **basketball**   **equestrian**   **taekwondo**

4. Circle the word that has a different first letter.

   ball   **wrestle**   **bat**   **boat**   **box**

5. Circle the word that has a different last letter.

   volleyball   **basketball**   **softball**   **handball**   **tennis**

6. Circle the word that has double consonants in it (as in *better*).

   diving   **playing**   **swimming**   **cycling**   **fencing**

7. Circle the word that begins with a vowel.

   archery   **water**   **field**   **target**   **kayak**

For younger students: Read each set of directions to the children. Have them write the number of letters under each word.

For older students: Highlight all the vowels in each word.

Shapes at the Olympic Games

Directions: Color all △s yellow.   _____

Color all ▭s blue.   _____

Color all ◯s red.   _____

For younger students: Count how many of each shape. Write the numbers on the lines at the top.

For older students: Count how many of each shape. Write the numbers on the lines at the top. Next to each picture, write the name of the sport.

Olympic Games Rhymes

Directions: Draw a line to match the pictures that rhyme.

Olympic Sport	Rhymes With

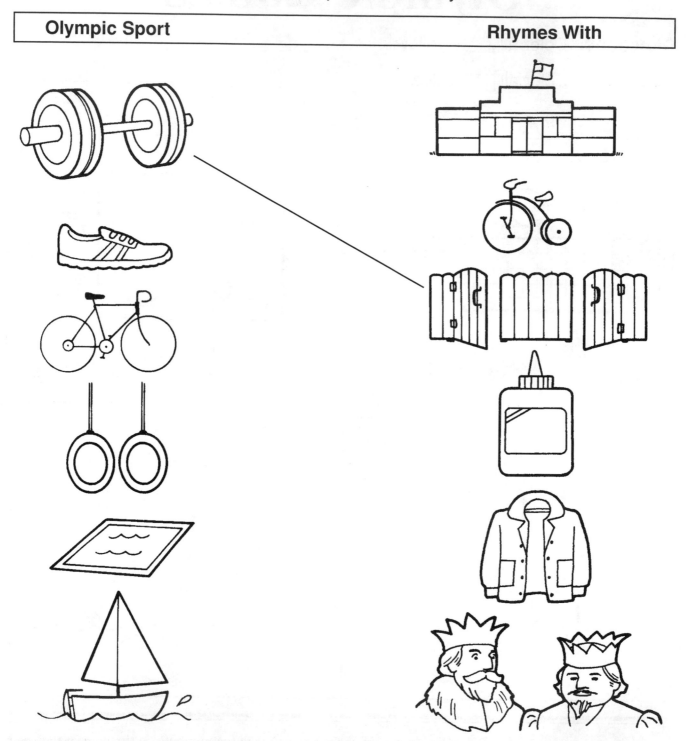

For younger students: Write the word next to the picture on the right side.
For older students: Write a new rhyming word next to the picture on the right side.

Olympic Games
Words A-B-C

Directions: Cut out the cards. Glue them in A-B-C order on another paper.

run	dive	box	row
run	dive	box	row
soccer	team	Olympics USA	swim
soccer	team	Olympics USA	swim

For younger students: Have the children cut the cards apart. Pair them and let them play "Go Fish."

For older students: Write a sentence on each card.

Olympic Games Equipment

Directions: Write the word for each picture. The words are in the word box.

Word Bank			
bat	racquet	gloves	ball

_____

_____

_____

_____

For younger students: Write a rhyming word next to each word in the box.

For older students: On the back of this paper, write a sentence for each picture using the word.

Olympic Games Sets

Directions: Cut out the pictures and words. Glue the three things that go together for each sport on another paper.

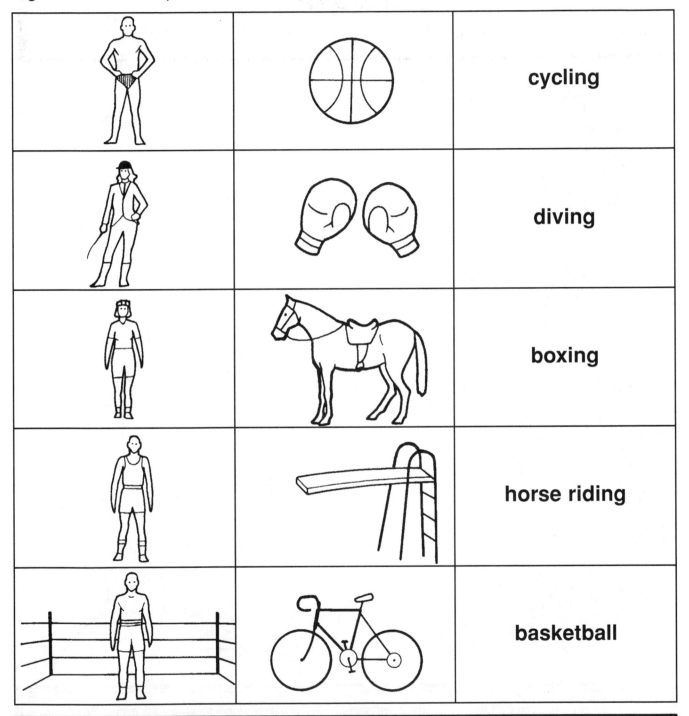

For younger students: Pair the students. Give each pair one paper and have the students work together to create the sets.

For older students: Under each set, write one sentence about the sport.

Whose Feet?

Directions: Draw a line to match the people to their feet.

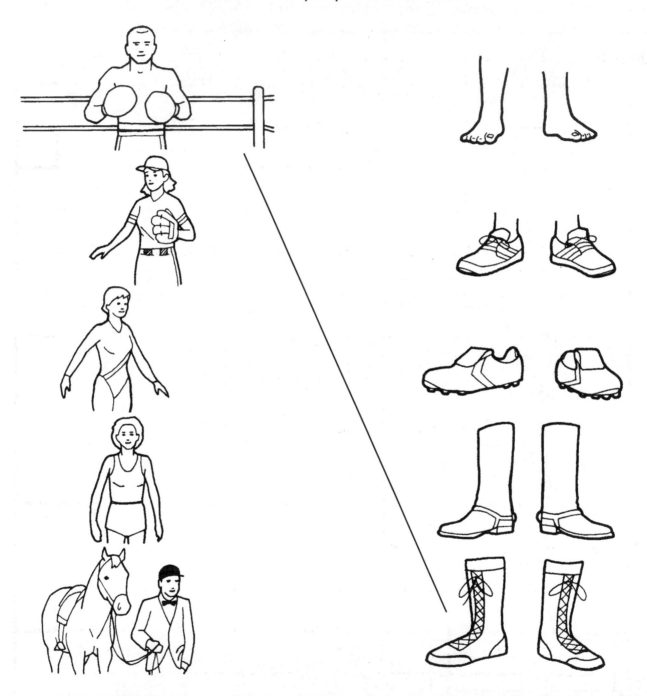

For younger students: Discuss with the students why athletes need to wear different things on their feet.

For older students: Think about the things you wear on your feet. Then write the answers to these questions: How many different kinds of things do you wear on your feet? What are they? Why do you need each kind?

Marathon Maze

The marathon is a foot race. Many people begin. It is so long, however, that not everyone finishes. A marathon is a little more than 26 miles (40 kilometers) long. Do you think that you could run that far?

Directions: Find the way through the maze for the marathon runner.

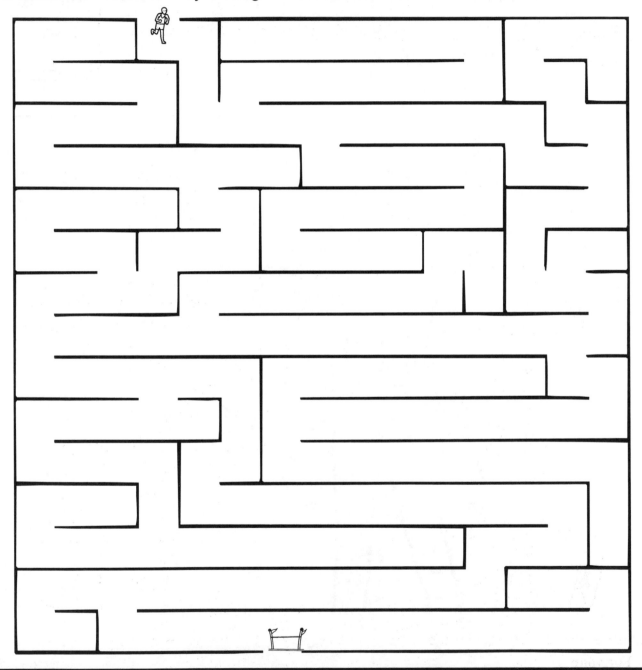

For younger students: Which is shorter: 26 miles or 50 kilometers? (Hint: read the paragraph above the maze.)

For older students: How is a marathon different from the 50-meter dash?

57

Complete the Diagram

Directions: Cut out the words. Glue the words at the end of the lines.

quiver	arrow	sight
bowstring	bow	wrist strap

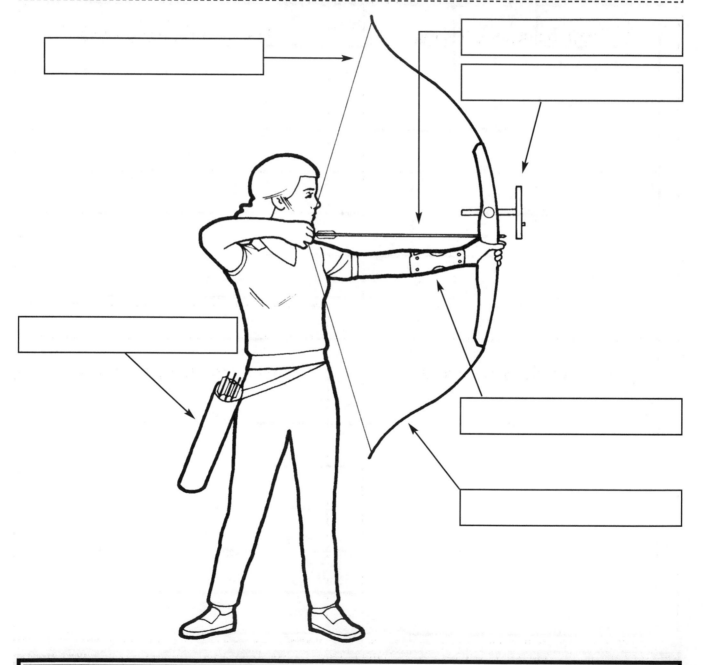

For younger students: Color the diagram.

For older students: Color the diagram. Draw lines and write labels for three of the archer's body parts.

Naming Words from the Olympic Games

Directions: In each box, draw a picture that matches the sentence.

The woman swings the bat.

The man rows the kayak.

The woman dives into the pool.

The man rides the horse.

For younger students: Underline the words that name a person or thing.

For older students: Underline the naming words (nouns). Then write "p" under words that name persons and "t" under words that name things.

Doing Words from the Olympic Games

Directions: In each box, draw a picture that matches the sentence.

The woman runs on the track.

The man rides a bike.

The woman jumps very far.

The man shoots an arrow.

For younger students: Underline the words that show what the person is doing.

For older students: Underline the doing words (verbs). Write a list of the doing words on the back of this paper.

Word Search Puzzle

Directions: Find the clues from the Word Bank in the puzzle. Circle them.

Word Bank

archery	handball	wrestle
tennis	kayak	swim

A	X	T	Q	N	K	G	W	A
B	Y	A	R	C	H	E	R	Y
C	K	U	R	O	L	H	E	B
D	A	T	E	N	N	I	S	C
E	Y	V	S	W	I	M	T	D
H	A	N	D	B	A	L	L	E
Z	K	W	S	P	M	J	E	F

1. What word has the most letters?_____

2. How many letters does it have?_____

3. What word has the least letters?_____

4. How many letters does it have?_____

For younger students: Answer the questions.

For older students: Answer the questions. Write the words from the word box in alphabetical order on the back of this paper.

Rebus Crossword Puzzle

Directions: Pick a word from the box to complete the clue.

Word Bank		
five	throw	dive
team	row	dream

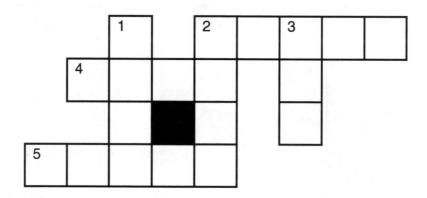

Across

2. He will _____ the 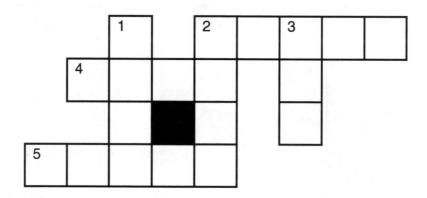 as far as he can.

4. She will _____ from a ____ .

5. They _____ of getting a ____ .

Down

1. There are _____ Olympic rings.

2. Each _____ wants to win.

3. She will _____ a ____ .

Words that Rhyme

_____ and _____

_____ and _____

_____ and _____

For younger students: Find the three pairs of words that rhyme.

For older students: Find the three pairs of words that rhyme. Write a sentence using each rhyming pair (for example: It is fun to run).

Finish the Picture

Directions: Draw the Olympic flag **behind** the pitcher.

Draw a softball **in** her right hand.

Draw a mitt **on** her left hand.

Draw a baseball cap **on** her head.

Write a number **on the front of** her uniform.

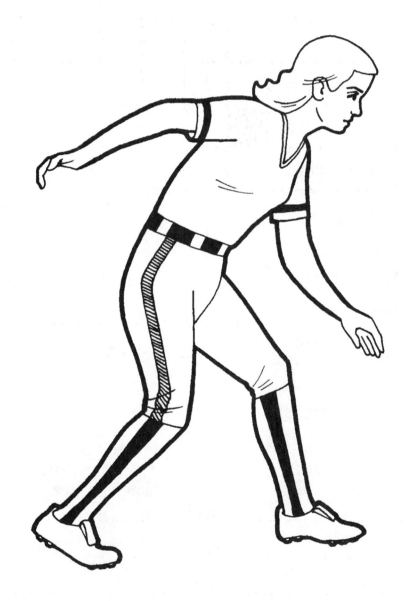

For younger students: Color the picture.

For older students: Write a 3- or 4-sentence story about the softball player.

Marathon Math

Directions: Solve. Show your work. Drawing pictures may help you to solve the problems. Answer with a number and a label.

1. _____ men start the 50-meter dash. Only _____ men finish it. How many more started than finished?

Answer: _____

2. It took the women's marathon winner _____ hours to finish the race. It took the last woman _____ hours to finish. What is the difference between their times?

Answer: _____

3. There are _____ runners in the 100-meter dash. How many total legs will run around the track?

Answer: _____

4. The Olympics begin on _____ and end on _____. Look at a calendar. Count the days. How many days long are the Olympics?

Answer: _____

5. There are _____ cyclists. How many total wheels are on their bicycles?

Answer: _____

6. _____ women will each throw a javelin three times. How many total times will a javelin be thrown by the women?

Answer: _____

Note to the teacher: Fill in the blanks with numbers that match your students' abilities.

Comparing Size and Weight

Directions: Use the picture letters to answer the questions.

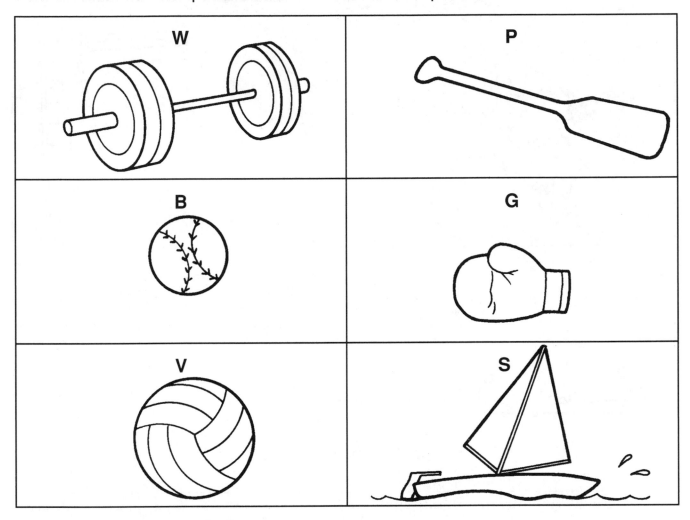

1. What thing is about the same size as a soccer ball? _____ _____

2. Which thing(s) could fit in a paper grocery bag? _____ _____

3. Which thing(s) does a person put on his or her body? _____ _____

4. Which thing is the longest? _____ _____

5. Which thing is the shortest? _____ _____

6. Which thing(s) are used in water? _____ _____

For younger students: Discuss the answers to the questions.

For older students: Answer the questions. On the second set of lines, list the things in order from smallest to biggest.

Time Sense

Directions: Color the picture in each set that takes **more time** to finish.

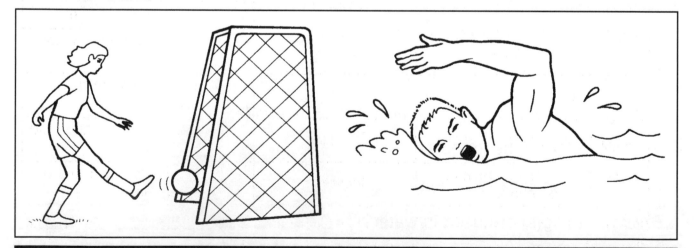

For younger students: Write man or woman under each picture.

For older students: For each pair of pictures, write a sentence telling which sport you like better and why.

Science Connection: Friction

1. Friction is a force trying to stop movement between any two surfaces. A lack of friction allows things to slide. Without friction, a person who started running couldn't stop. A person wouldn't be able to pick up or kick a ball because it would slip away. Some friction is essential for most of the sports in the Olympic Games.

2. To help children learn about friction, freeze a thin layer of water in a cookie sheet. Have the children take turns trying to slide a penny across the ice in the cookie sheet, across a piece of carpeting, across a piece of sandpaper, and across their desktops. When they discover that the penny glides the most easily (and farthest) on the ice, explain about friction. Ask your students:

   • What had the most friction? Why do you think this is?

   • What other surface had a lot of friction? Why do you think this is?

   • What had the least friction? Why do you think this is?

3. Demonstrate to the students how difficult life would be without any friction. Close a door and smear the doorknob with lotion. Ask the children to try to open the door.

4. Screw the lid on a glass jar. Smear the lid with petroleum jelly. Ask the children to try to open the jar.

5. Sometimes Olympic athletes want to increase friction and other times they want to decrease it. Ask the children the questions in this chart. The answers are provided for your convenience.

Think about . . .	Used to increase or decrease friction?	Why is that useful in this sport?
soccer cleats	increase	helps player to not slip when chasing ball
swim cap	decrease	helps swimmer glide through water quickly
tight fitting running clothes	decrease	cuts down on wind resistance so runner goes faster
baseball cleats	increase	helps player to not slip when running
oiling bike wheels	decrease	lets wheels spin easily so biker can go fast
soccer goalee wearing gloves	increase	helps goalee to catch and hold the ball
gymnasts putting chalk on their hands	increase	gives gymnasts better grip on bars

6. Show the students how friction generates heat by having them rub two sticks together rapidly, and then feel the sticks in the places where they rubbed. Expand on this concept by discussing times when people use friction to warm up (rubbing hands together when cold) or do things to decrease friction (grease the moving parts of bicycles, car doors, truck motors, etc.). Another friction-causing-heat example they'll probably understand is the smell of burning rubber or the sight of skid marks caused when vehicle tires skid on pavement.

Skating at the Olympic Winter Games

Directions: Cut out the pictures. Glue them on another paper in the right order.*

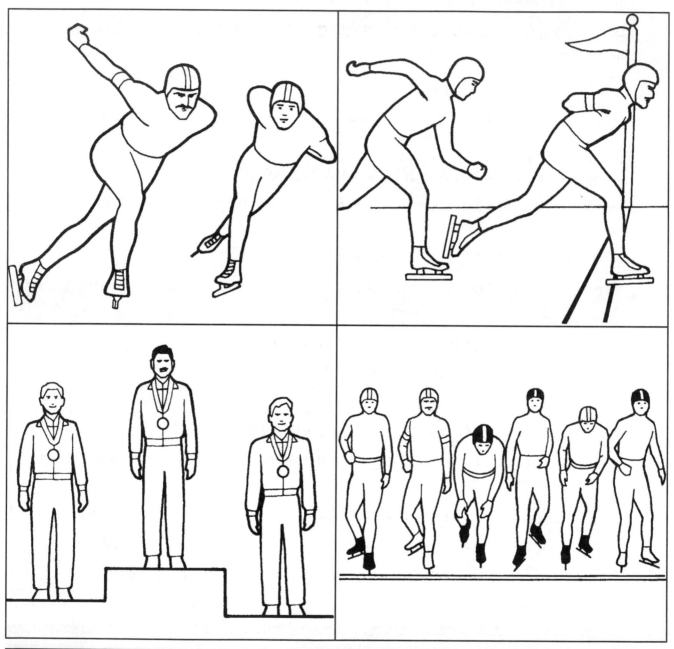

For younger students: Write a caption under each picture.

For older students: Write four sentences that tell the story in the order in which it happened.

*You may prefer to have the children use these pages to create a mini book.

Words from the Olympic Winter Games

Directions: Count the letters in each word.

1. Circle the longest word.

   biathlon   **snowboard**   **curling**   **skiing**   **hockey**

2. Circle the shortest word.

   bobsled   **puck**   **goal**   **ski**   **skates**

3. Circle the word that has a different number of letters.

   luge   **curl**   **speed**   **ride**   **skis**

4. Circle the word that has a different first letter.

   skate   **sled**   **ski**   **luge**   **snowboard**

5. Circle the word that has a different last letter.

   bobsled   **snowboard**   **speed**   **raced**   **curl**

6. Circle the word that has a double consonant (as in *better*).

   snowboarding   **bobsledding**   **shooting**   **skiing**   **speeding**

7. Circle the word that begins with a vowel.

   ice   **skate**   **puck**   **goal**   **stick**

For younger students: Read each set of directions to the children. Have them write the number of letters under each word.

For older students: Highlight all the vowels in each word.

Shapes at the Olympic Winter Games

Directions: Color all the ⬤ s red. _____

Color all the △ s yellow. _____

Color all the ▭ s blue. _____

For younger students: Count how many of each shape. Write the numbers on the lines at the top.

For older students: Count how many of each shape. Write the numbers on the lines at the top. Then write the name of the sport next to or under each picture.

Olympic Winter Games Rhymes

Directions: Draw a line to match the pictures that rhyme.

Olympic Equipment	Rhymes With

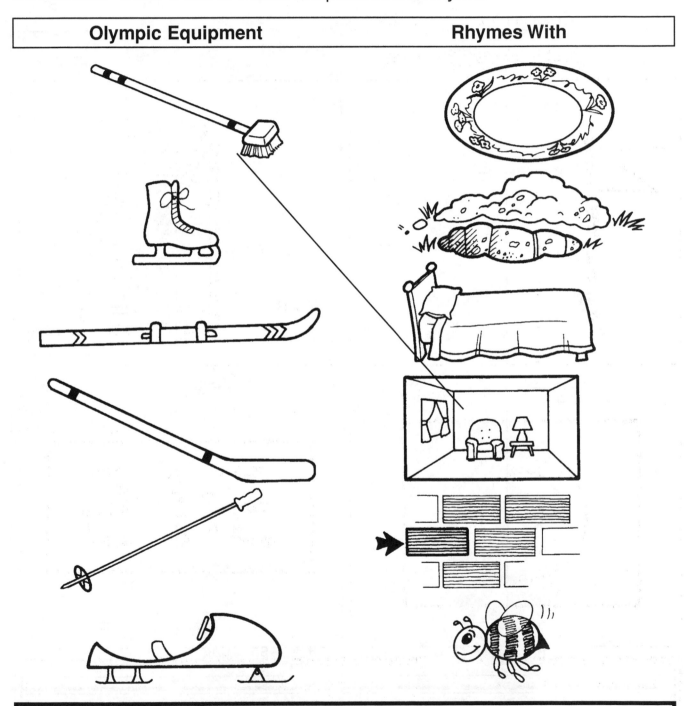

For younger students: Write the word next to the picture on the right side.

For older students: Write a new rhyming word next to the picture on the right side.

Olympic Winter Games
Words A-B-C

Directions: Cut out the cards. Glue them in A-B-C order on another paper.

curl	skate	bobsled	luge
curl	skate	bobsled	luge
ski	team	Olympics **USA**	hockey
ski	team	Olympics **USA**	hockey

For younger students: Have the children cut the cards apart. Pair them and let them play "Go Fish."

For older students: Write a sentence on each card.

Olympic Winter Games Equipment

Directions: Write the word for each picture. The words are in the word box.

Word Bank			
ski	sled	snowboard	skate

_____

_____

_____

_____

For younger students: Write a rhyming word next to each word in the box.

For older students: On the back of this paper write a sentence for each picture using the word from the box.

73

Olympic Winter Games Sets

Directions: Cut out the pictures and words. Glue the three things that go together for each sport on another paper.

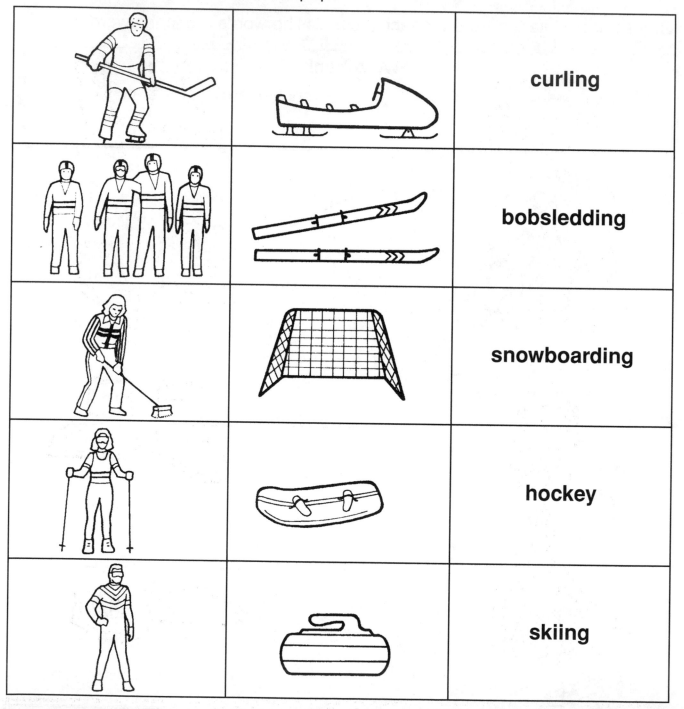

		curling
		bobsledding
		snowboarding
		hockey
		skiing

For younger students: Pair the students. Give each pair one paper and have the students work together to create the sets.

For older students: Under each set, write one sentence about the sport.

Whose Feet?

Directions: Draw a line to match the people to their feet.

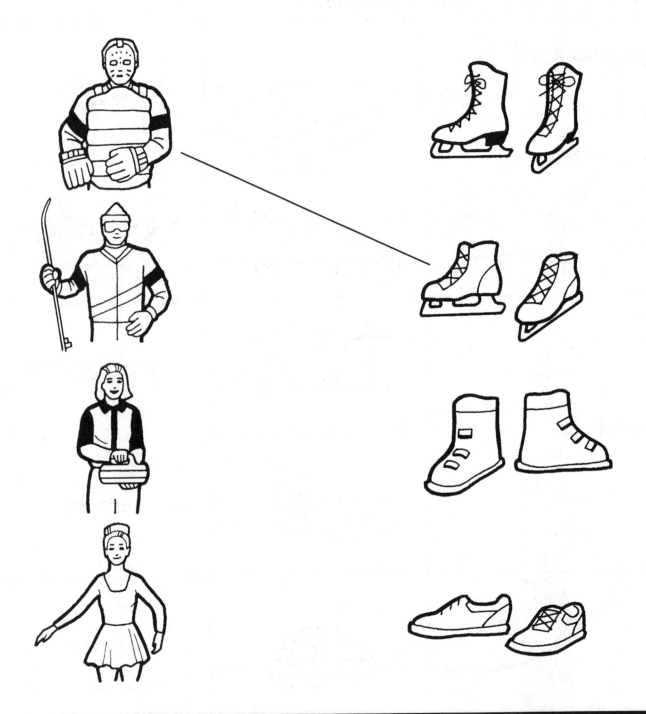

For younger students: Discuss with the children why athletes need to wear different things on their feet.

For older students: Think about the things you wear on your feet. How many different kinds of things do you wear on your feet? Why do you need each kind?

Luge Maze

The luge is a kind of sled. A person lies down on it. Then the sled slides down an icy track that has lots of turns. The person who gets to the bottom the fastest wins.

Directions: Find the way through the maze.

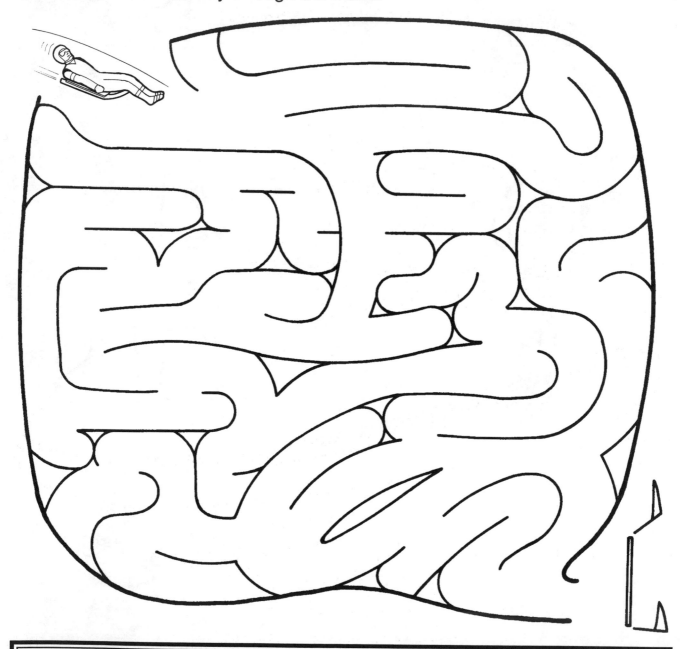

For younger students: Draw your own maze on the back of this paper. Can your friends find their way through?

For older students: Draw your own maze on the back of this paper. Can your friends find their way through? What other Olympic Winter Games event uses a track like the one a luge uses?

Complete the Diagram

Directions: Cut out the words. Glue the words at the end of the lines.

handle	runner	axle
cowling		helmet

For younger students: Color the diagram.
For older students: Color the diagram. Write a short story about the bobsled team's race.

Naming Words from the Olympic Winter Games

Directions: In each box, draw a picture that matches the sentence.

The woman wears skates.	The man rides a snowboard.
The team goes down the bobsled course.	The woman sweeps the ice with a broom.

For younger students: Underline the words that name a person or thing.

For older students: Underline the naming words (nouns). Write "p" under words that name person and "t" under words that name things.

Doing Words from the Olympic Winter Games

Directions: In each box, draw a picture that matches the sentence.

The man rides on a luge.

The woman skis down the hill.

The hockey player makes a goal.

The man and woman skate well.

For younger students: Underline the words that show what the person is doing.

For older students: Underline the doing words (verbs). Write a list of the doing words on the back of this paper.

Word Search Puzzle

Directions: Find the clues from the Word Bank in the puzzle. Circle them.

Word Bank

bobsled	luge	snowboard
ski	skate	hockey

```
S   N   O   W   B   O   A   R   D
K   Z   B   C   O   D   E   F   G
A   I   J   A   B   L   M   N   O
T   Q   R   B   S   T   U   V   W
E   Y   Z   S   L   U   G   E   B
H   O   C   K   E   Y   D   E   F
H   I   J   I   D   M   N   O   P
```

1. What word has the most letters? _____

2. How many letters does it have? _____

3. What word has the least letters? _____

4. How many letters does it have? _____

For younger students: Answer the questions.
For older students: Answer the questions. Write the words from the word box in alphabetical order on the back of this paper.

Rebus Crossword Puzzle

Directions: Pick a word from the box to complete the clue.

Word Bank

poles	gold	cold
dreams	teams	goals

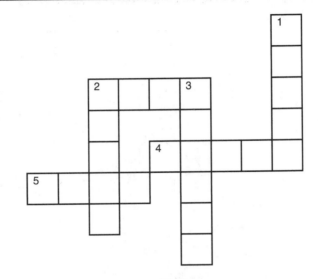

Across

2. The best 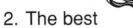 is _____ .

4. The  _____ want to win.

5. The Winter Games are held when it is _____ .

Down

1. A  needs two _____ .

2. Hockey players hit a to make _____ .

3. Everyone _____ of winning a .

Words that Rhyme

_____ and _____

_____ and _____

_____ and _____

For younger students: Find the three pairs of words that rhyme.

For older students: Find the three pairs of words that rhyme. Write a silly sentence using each rhyming pair (for example, It is fun to run).

Finish the Picture

Directions: Draw the Olympic flag **behind** the skier.

Draw skis **below** the skier.

Draw ski poles **in** his hands.

Draw ski boots **on** his feet.

For younger students: Color the picture.

For older students: Write a 3- or 4-sentence story about the cross-country skier.

Winter Events Math

Directions: Solve. Show your work. Drawing pictures may help you to solve the problems. Answer with a number and a label.

1. There are 4 women on a bobsled team. There are _____ teams. How many women are in the bobsled event? Answer: _____	4. The Olympics begins on _____ and ends on _____. Look at a calendar. Count the days. How many days long are the Olympics? Answer: _____
2. It took the women's cross-country ski winner _____ hours to finish the race. It took the last woman _____ hours to finish. What's the difference between their times? Answer: _____	5. There are _____ high jump skiers. How many total skis are they wearing? Answer: _____
3. _____ U.S. figure skaters will skate in _____ events. How many total skating events will the U.S. skaters be in? Answer: _____	6. There are _____ skaters in the 100-meter race. How many total legs will skate around the tack? Answer: _____

Note to the teacher: Fill in the blanks with numbers that match your students' abilities.

Comparing Size and Weight

Directions: Use the picture letters to answer the questions.

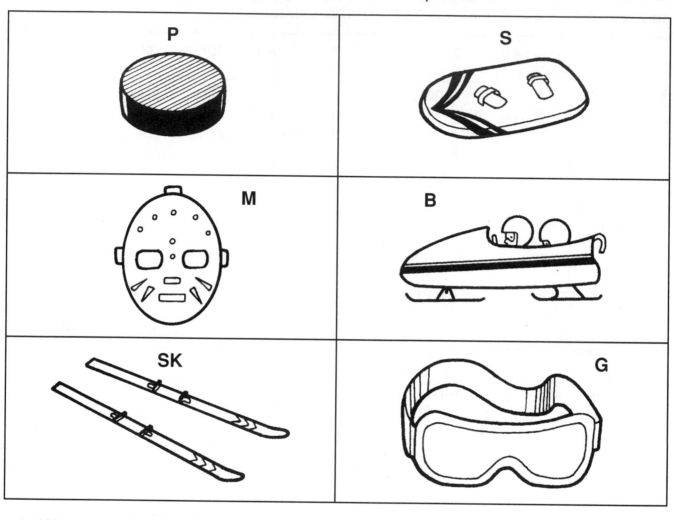

1. What thing is about the same size as skateboard? _____ _____

2. Which thing(s) could fit in your pocket? _____ _____

3. Which thing(s) does a person put on his body? _____ _____

4. Which thing is the longest? _____ _____

5. Which thing is the shortest? _____ _____

6. Which thing(s) could fit in a paper grocery bag? _____ _____

For younger students: Discuss the answers to the questions.

For older students: Answer the questions. On the second set of lines use the numbers to list the things in order from smallest to biggest.

Time Sense

Directions: Color the picture in each set that takes less time to finish.

For younger students: Write man or woman under each picture.

For older students: Write a sentence for each pair of pictures telling which sport you like better and why.

Science Connection: Ice

Water is one of the few known substances that can exist as a gas (vapor), liquid, and solid. Water in its solid form (snow or ice) is essential for all the Olympic Winter Games. Here are a few activities to do with your students to help them to understand concepts about ice.

1. Ask the students what happens when water freezes (it turns to ice). Explain that ice takes up less space than water, so it floats—but just barely. For example, there is nine times more ice beneath a floating iceberg than what shows above the water. Prove this to your students by placing one ice cube in a clear glass full of water.

2. Ask the children to predict what will happen when the ice cube melts (most will think the glass will overflow). Set the glass with ice aside and check it later in the day when the ice has completely melted. Explain that it did not overflow because the water from the ice takes up less space than the ice cube did.

3. Ice is a unique solid because of its lack of friction. This lack of friction allows things to slide and is a requirement for all sports of the Olympic Winter Games. To demonstrate this, freeze a thin layer of water in a cookie sheet. Have the children take turns trying to slide a penny across the ice in the cookie sheet, across a piece of carpeting, across a piece of sandpaper, and across their desktops. When they discover that the penny glides the most easily (and farthest) on the ice, explain about friction. Friction is a force trying to stop movement between any two surfaces.

   Ask your students:

   - What had the most friction? Why do you think this is?

   - What other surface had a lot of friction? Why do you think this is?

   - What had the least friction? Why do you think this is?

4. Children may question you about the difference between ice and frost. When liquid water freezes, it forms ice. When water vapor in the air freezes, it forms snowflakes. When snowflakes harden on an object, it forms frost (like what you find inside a freezer or on a window on a cold day).

5. You may also want to explain how icicles form: Snow (usually on a roof) melts on a warm or sunny day. The water runs down the roof and drips off the edge. When the temperature drops (often at night), the dripping water hardens into icicles.

6. When something heavy moves across ice, its weight pushing down on the ice makes it temporarily melt. This reduces friction and enables skaters, bobsled runners, and luge sleds to glide over the ice quickly. The ice melts under the runners of the skates or sled. As soon as the weight passes over, the ice refreezes. Demonstrate this principle to your students by obtaining two identical pieces of metal silverware, a thin, strong string, a bottle with a tight-fitting cork, and a large ice cube. Push the cork into the bottle's neck until about 1 inch (2.5 cm) sticks up. Place the ice cube on top of the cork. Then cut a piece of string about one foot (30 cm) long. Attach a piece of silverware to each end of the string. Hang the string on top of the ice cube. Place the bottle in the fridge. The string will eventually pass through the ice cube; yet the ice cube will not be split in two. Lift the ice cube, and the students will see that the string is balanced on top of the cork. They'll think it's magic, but you can explain that the silverware's weight temporarily melted the ice beneath it. As soon as the string moved through an area, the ice refroze above it.

Junior Olympic Games

Your students will have fun staging their own Junior Olympic Games. Here are some suggestions. Have the children prepare the medals for which they will compete (see page 89).

Have your students help you to measure distances. Briefly discuss the metric system and why it is used in the Olympics. (Almost every other world nation uses it.)

Opening Ceremony

Put the students into alphabetical order. Have the class march quietly around the school corridors. The leader should carry a torch held high. (You can make a torch by fastening a crumpled piece of orange tissue paper inside an empty paper towel tube.) The second child in line should carry the American flag.

When they reach the site of the Games, lead the children in reciting the Olympic Oath, pausing at each comma so that they can repeat after you:

> *In the name of all competitors, I promise that we shall take part in these Olympic Games, respecting and abiding by the rules which govern them, in the true spirit of sportsmanship, for the glory of the sport, and the honor of our teams.*

If you can, play the Olympic theme song: *World Anthems* performed by Donald Fraser, English Chamber Orchestra. Audio CD (1 disc). BMG/RCA Victor, 63231, 1998. AISN: B000007QGU.

Events

Enlist your physical education teacher's help in selecting, scheduling, and doing events. Here are some ideas:

- baseball game (using plastic balls and bats)
- basketball game (using reduced-size balls and small, plastic hoops)
- volleyball game
- soccer game
- 50-meter dash (race run on a measured track)—Each child should run and be timed individually. Use a stopwatch.
- 100-meter relay (team of four pass an unsharpened pencil while running on a measured track)
- discus throw (throw a frisbee)—Each participant will have three tries at throwing the frisbee; count only the longest throw for each.
- long jump (a measured jump from a standing or running position; best done on sand or grass)—Each participant will have three tries at jumping from a scratch line; count only the longest jump for each.

Junior Olympic Games *(cont.)*

Events *(cont.)*

- high jump (child stands next to a wall with a piece of colored chalk in hand, then jumps up as high as possible, marking on the wall with the chalk)—Each participant will have three tries at jumping; count only the highest jump for each.

- javelin throw (throw a rigid, plastic drinking straw)—Each participant will have three tries at throwing the javelin; count only the longest throw for each.

- shot-put (throw a foam ball)—Each participant will have three tries at throwing the shot-put; count only the longest throw for each.

Decide if you want students to sign up to participate in one or two events. Based on the physical education teacher's knowledge of your children's abilities, guide the students to choose events in which he or she will probably be successful.

Ask for adult volunteers to do measuring and recording of scores.

If you are concerned about children not winning a medal, have only three children participate in each of the six individual track events (18 children). In this way, they are guaranteed to win one of the three medals for each event.

Medal Ceremony

Have the gold medal winner stand on a chair with the silver and bronze medalists standing on the floor on either side. Play the American national anthem as you solemnly place the medals over each child's head (do bronze first, silver second, and gold third).

Closing Ceremony

Copy the certificate on page 90. Hand out certificates to all the children who did not receive medals. Remind them that even though they did not receive a medal, they are still Olympians.

If you can, play the Olympic theme song: *World Anthems* performed by Donald Fraser, English Chamber Orchestra. Audio CD (1 disc). BMG/RCA Victor, 63231, 1998. AISN: B000007QGU.

Proud Participant
in the

Junior Olympic Games

U S A

36 USC 380

Athlete's Name: _____Kenneth Chan_____
Event: _____high jump_____ Date: May 12, 2002
Teacher/Coach: _____Mr. Bolton_____

Medals

1. Reproduce the medal pattern below. You may want to prepare a model to show the students.

2. Assign one third of your class to design a gold medal, another third to design a silver medal, and the remaining third to design a bronze medal. Each medal must have the word "gold," "silver," or bronze," but must not be colored. They should draw their designs using a regular pencil.

3. Have the children sort the medals into their color groups. Post all the medals around the classroom.

4. Ask the children to study the medals carefully; they are going to vote for their favorite in each category.

5. Hold a class vote for the favorite gold, favorite silver, and favorite bronze medals. This is an ideal opportunity to explain the use of tally marks and the democratic process (majority vote).

6. Take the favorite medal from each category and glue it to a piece of paper.

7. Trace over the medal designs with a black, felt-tip marker.

8. Make copies of the page for each event you have in your Junior Olympics.

9. Put the medal photocopies in a learning center. Ask the children to cut them out and glue them to oaktag. They should then color the medals appropriately. Be sure to provide gold, silver, and bronze crayons in the learning center for this purpose.

10. Paper punch a hole in the top of each medal and thread a grossgrain ribbon about 24" (61 cm) long through the hole. Award these medals to the top three competitors in each Junior Olympics event.

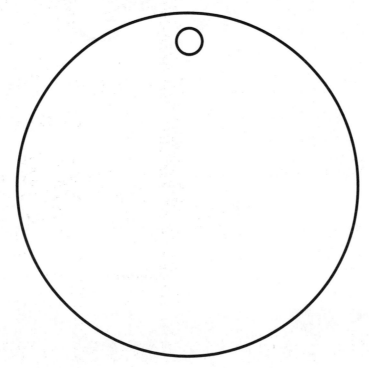

Student Certificate

Proud Participant
in the

Junior Olympic Games

U S A

36 USC 380

Athlete's Name: _____

Event: _____ Date: _____

Teacher/Coach: _____

The Paralympic Games

In 1960 four hundred athletes from 23 different countries gathered in Rome for the first Paralympic Games. Ever since then the Paralympic Games have been held every four years immediately following the Olympic Games or Olympic Winter Games. The vision for the Paralympics came from an English doctor who worked with many World War II veterans suffering from spinal cord injuries. Dr. Ludwig Guttman wanted a world-class event that would put the spotlight on physically disabled athletes.

Paralympics means "parallel to" or "next to" the Olympic Games. From the opening ceremony to the closing ceremony, the Paralympics mirror the Olympics they follow. They often use the same facilities. World-class, well-trained disabled athletes are selected to represent their countries based on their performances in qualifying events. As in the Olympics, the top Paralympic performers receive gold, silver, and bronze medals. The Paralympics are not the Special Olympics, in which all the participants receive medals.

Minor modifications may be made to the rules of each sport to accommodate some of the athletes' disabilities. Athletes are classified according to the severity of their disabilities. Then they compete against athletes with similar disabilities. The people who participate in the Paralympic Games have disabilities such as:

- blindness or visual impairment
- cerebral palsy
- amputation (having a limb partially or completed removed)
- dwarfism
- paraplegics (having legs that are partially or totally paralyzed)
- quadriplegics (having arms and legs that are partially or totally paralyzed)

More than 4,000 athletes participated at the Sydney Paralympic Games in 2000. They competed in 18 different events, most of which are also on the Olympic program. Sailing and Wheelchair Rugby were the new events in 2000.

The Paralympics Summer Sports Program

Archery	Goalball	Swimming
Athletics (Track & Field)	Judo	Table Tennis
Basketball	Lawn Bowling	Tennis
Boccia	Powerlifting	Volleyball
Cycling	Sailing	Wheelchair Rugby
Equestrian	Shooting	
Fencing	Soccer	

The Paralympics Winter Sports Program

Biathlon	Alpine Skiing
Ice Hockey	Cross-Country Skiing
Speed Skating	

Bibliography

Anderson, Dave. *The Story of the Olympics*. HarperCollins Juvenile Books, 2000. This very informative book includes a lot of photographs and covers both summer and winter Olympic events.

Bauer, Larry. *Easy Olympic Sports Readers*. Teacher Created Materials, 1998. This set of six short, full-color books provides beginning readers with an excellent introduction to the events in the Olympic Winter Games (i.e., skiing, speed skating, figure skating, sledding, snowboarding, and ice hockey).

Crowther, Robert. *Robert Crowther's Pop-Up Olympics: Amazing Facts and Record Breakers*. Candlewick Press, 1996. This delightful book about the Summer Games has pull tabs that let children make athletes swim, throw basketballs in a hoop, and straddle parallel bars.

Hennessy, B. G. *Olympics!* Viking Penguin Books, 1996. This easy-reader picture book gives a brief history of the Olympics and provides an interesting overview of the events in both the Olympic Games and the Olympic Winter Games.

Holzschuler, Cynthia. *United States Olympic Committee's Curriculum Guide to the Olympic Games: The Olympic Dream*. Griffin Publishing Group/Teacher Created Materials, Inc., 2000. This teacher resource book is filled with activities for advanced primary students.

Ledeboer, Suzanne. *Olympism: A Basic Guide to the History, Ideals, and Sports of the Olympic Movement*. Griffin Publishing Group, 2001. This guide, which explains the history and rules of each Olympic Sport, would prove helpful in answering student queries while doing pocket chart or felt board activities that introduce Olympic events.

Osborne, Mary Pope. *Hour of the Olympics*. Random House, 1998. This is a title in the Magic Tree House easy reader beginning chapter book series. In the story, Annie and Jack are transported through time back to the first ancient Olympic Games.

Oxlade, Chris and David Ballheimer. *Eyewitness: Olympics*. Dorling Kindersley Publishing, Inc., 2000. Like all Eyewitness books, this volume is loaded with detailed photographs and fascinating trivia. It includes a section on the Paralympics.

The following are from the True Book Series, a set of short, factual books filled with color photos and large print just right for reading aloud to students. Some adept students may be able to read these themselves.

Brimmer, Larry Dane. *Bobsledding & the Luge*. School & Library Binding, 1997. (Grades K-3)

————. *The Winter Olympics*. School & Library Binding, 1997. (Grades K–3)

Ditchfield, Christin. *Cycling*. Children's Press, 2000. (Grades K–3)

————. *Gymnastics*. Children's Press, 2000. (Grades K–3)

————. *Kayaking, Canoeing, and Yachting*. Children's Press, 2000. (Grades K–3)

————. *Swimming and Diving*. Children's Press, 2000. (Grades K–3)

————. *Wrestling*. Children's Press, 2000. (Grades K–3)

Knotts, Bob. *Equestrian Events*. Children's Press, 2000. (Grades K–3)

————. *Martial Arts*. Children's Press, 2000. (Grades K–3)

————. *The Summer Olympics*. Children's Press, 2000. (Grades K–3) Includes brief history of the Olympic Games.

————. *Track & Field*. Children's Press, 2000. (Grades K–3)

————. *Weightlifting*. Children's Press, 2000. (Grades K–3)

Web Sites

For Students

www.sikids.com—This *Sports Illustrated* site was ranked one of the top kids sites in Yahoo Internet Life's 100 Best Sites of 2000. It features sports trivia, news, sports arcade games, and fantasy leagues. There is also a link for teachers in underfunded districts to get access to free teaching materials.

www.timeforkids.com—This site offers the latest information on recent or upcoming Olympic events.

members.aol.com/msdaizy/sports/locker.html—This site lets children learn more about their favorite sports, offers advice on how to work out problems with teammates, and provides sports-related online games.

For Teachers

www.edgate.com/school_athletics/educator—This site offers links to various Olympic- and sports-related sites.

www.education-world.com/a_sites/sites047.shtml—This is Education World's Great Sites for Teaching About the Olympics. It offers links to 10 sites that offer free lesson plans.

www.nbcolympics.com—This site offers daily news updates on the Olympics, medal totals, and individual athletes.

www.olympics.org—This Web site belongs to the International Olympics Committee (IOC). It offers the latest information on the current and upcoming Olympics. However, much of the information is in the language of the host country.

www.olympics.usatoday.com—This site has animated graphics that explain curling. If you click on "Student Gateway to the Games," you can get lesson plans and explore past host countries, plus obtain fun facts and news for kids.

www.saltlake2002.com—This is the official Web site for the Salt Lake City 2002 Games. At this site, choose "For Kids." When you reach the "For Kids" screen, click on "Select a Category." Included is an explanation of the Native American folklore behind the 2002 mascot choices. You can also print out a coloring book and word puzzles for children.

www.usoc.org—This is the Web site of the United States Olympic Committee (USOC). You can sign up for a free e-newsletter or search news archives for articles about specific athletes or events.

www.washingtonpost.com/wp-dyn/sports/leaguesandsports/olympics/—This site has in-depth coverage of current Olympics and extensive news archives on past Olympics.

Answer Key

page 28
1. Olympia, Greece
2. 776 B.C.E., or almost 3,000 years ago
3. men and boys
4. chariot races, foot races, throwing spears, throwing discs, boxing, long jump, and wrestling (any three)
5. a crown of olive leaves, fame and honor, parties

page 33
Ring colors from left to right: blue, yellow, black, green, red. The Olympic ring colors were chosen because they represent at least one color from each participating nation's flag.

page 40
Italy—2

Canada—4

Japan—5

Great Britain—3

Mexico— 6

Greece—1

page 44
Under Olympic Winter Games:

curling broom w/rock—C

ski w/poles—S

ice skate—S

Under Olympic Games:

baseball—B

javelin—J

bicycle—B

page 46
1. 12	4. 10	7. 16	10. 16
2. 14	5. 13	8. 17	11. 11
3. 11	6. 11	9. 18	12. 15

Go For The Gold

page 47
1. 0	8. 2	15. 6
2. 8	9. 1	16. 1
3. 1	10. 10	17. 2
4. 4	11. 4	18. 1
5. 3	12. 8	19. 3
6. 5	13. 9	20. 2
7. 7	14. 5	

Swifter, Higher, Stronger

page 48
Color January and February blue; color July, August, and September yellow. Winter events are held in winter months in the Northern hemisphere so that there is enough snow and ice. Summer events are held during summer months so there is no snow or ice.

page 49
1—women at the starting blocks

2—women running on the track

3—woman breaking the finish tape

4—three women on the medal podium

page 50
1. gymnastics	5. tennis
2. row	6. swimming
3. taekwondo	7. archery
4. wrestle	

page 51
2 rectangles: volleyball net, basketball backboard

4 triangles: two formed by wires on uneven parallel bars and sailboat's 2 sails

2 circles: volleyball, basketball

page 52
shoe, glue

bicycle, tricycle

gymnastic rings, kings

pool, school

sailboat, coat

page 53
box	run
dive	soccer
Olympics	swim
row	team

page 54
gloves	ball
bat	racquet

page 56

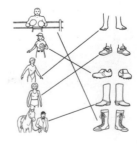

94

Answer Key *(cont.)*

page 57

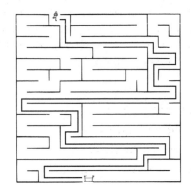

page 58

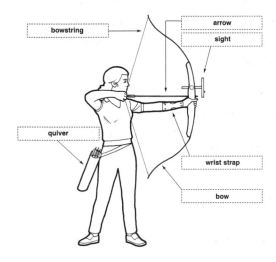

bowstring

arrow

sight

quiver

wrist strap

bow

page 59

1. woman (p), bat (t)
2. man (p), kayak (t)
3. woman (p), pool (t)
4. man (p), horse (t)

page 60

1. runs
2. rides
3. jumps
4. shoots

page 61

A	X	T	Q	N	K	G	W	A
B	Y	A	R	C	H	E	R	Y
C	K	U	R	O	L	H	E	B
D	A	T	E	N	N	I	S	C
E	Y	V	S	W	I	M	T	D
H	A	N	D	B	A	L	L	E
Z	K	W	S	P	M	J	E	F

1. What word has the most letters? __handball__
2. How many letters does it have? __8__
3. What word has the least letters? __swim__
4. How many letters does it have? __4__

page 62

Down

1. five
2. team
3. row

Across

2. throw
4. dive
5. dream

Rhyming Pairs

five, dive

team, dream

throw, row

page 64

Answers will vary.

page 65

1. V
2. B, V, G
3. G
4. S
5. B
6. P, S

Smallest to Biggest: B, G, V, P, W, S

page 66

These should be colored: cyclist, kayak team, swimmer.

page 68

1—men at the starting line

2—men racing around curve

3—man crossing finish line

4—three men on the medal podium

page 69

1. snowboard
2. ski
3. speed
4. luge
5. curl
6. bobsledding
7. ice

page 70

4 circles: puck, 3 target rings

2 triangles: ski flag, side of hockey goal

2 rectangles: digital timing clock, target board

Answer Key *(cont.)*

page 71

skate, plate

ski, bee

hockey stick, brick

ski pole, hole

bobsled, bed

page 72

bobsled

curl

hockey

luge

Olympics

skate

ski

team

page 73

skate

ski

sled

snowboard

page 75

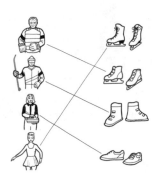

page 76

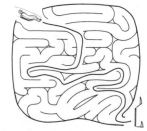

page 77

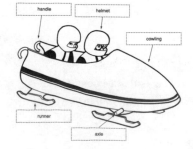

page 78

1. woman (p), skates (t)
2. man (p), snowboard (t)
3. team (t), bobsled, (t), course (t)
4. woman (p), ice (t), broom (t)

page 79

1. rides
2. skis
3. makes
4. skate

page 80

S	N	O	W	B	O	A	R	D
K	Z	B	C	O	D	E	F	G
A	I	J	A	B	L	M	N	O
T	Q	R	B	S	T	U	V	W
E	Y	Z	S	L	U	G	E	B
H	O	C	K	E	Y	D	E	F
H	I	J	I	D	M	N	O	P

1. What word has the most letters? **snowboard**
2. How many letters does it have? **9**
3. What word has the least letters? **ski**
4. How many letters does it have? **3**

page 81

Down

1. poles
2. goals
3. dreams

Across

2. gold
4. teams
5. cold

Rhyming Pairs

goals, poles

dreams, teams

gold, cold

page 84

1. S
2. P
3. M, S, G, SK
4. B
5. P
6. P, M, G

Smallest to Biggest: P, G, M, S, SK, B

page 85

These should be colored: hockey goal, luge, ski jumper.